AF351614

1939-1945
WORLD WAR TWO

AUTORE

Salvo Fagone was born in Catania in 1979, the city where he graduated in Computer Science at the University of Catania. He has always been a scholar of ancient and modern history, and in 2016 he began a collaboration with the DPAA, an institution of the U.S. Department of Defense that deals with the search for soldiers missing in war. During the years he has conducted research at the archives of the AFHRA, at Maxwell AFB, in Alabama, at the NARA in Washington DC, in the United States of America, and also in Canada, at the Library and Archives Canada (LAC), in England, at The National Archives (TNA) in Kew, in the French archives Le Service Historique de l'Armée de l'Air (SHAA), in the German Bundesarchiv and in the New Zealand archives of Auckland. He has written articles for various national and international periodicals. In October 2019, he published his first work, entitled "Reconnaissance over Husky. The Crucial Role of Air Reconnaissance and Ultra Intelligence over Sicily and the Mediterranean. 1940-1943".

PUBLISHING'S NOTES

LICENSES COMMONS

For a complete list of Soldiershop titles please contact Luca Cristini Editore on our website: www.soldiershop.com or www.cristinieditore.com. E-mail: info@soldiershop.com

On the cover : Some B-25 Mitchells have just attacked targets near Terni. B-17s attacked the city on August 11 and 28, and October 21, 1943. The last American bombing raid on Terni was carried out on April 24, 1944, by aircraft of the Tactical Air Force.

Title: **USAAF BOMBS ON ITALY** Code.: **WTW-029 ENG** By Salvo Fagone
ISBN code: 978-88-93278089 prima edizione Dicembre 2021
English text Nr. of images: 111 Layout: 177,8x254mm Cover & Art Design: Luca S. Cristini

WITNESS TO WAR (SOLDIERSHOP) is a trademark of Luca Cristini Editore, via Orio, 35/4 - 24050 Zanica (BG) ITALY.

WITNESS TO WAR

USAAF BOMBS ON ITALY

PHOTOS & IMAGES FROM WORLD WARTIME ARCHIVES

SALVO FAGONE

CONTENTS

▲ Bombing damage in Ostiense, Rome.

INTRODUCTION

The following book is a synthesis of the contribution of the American Air Force in the Mediterranean area, but especially in Italy, between 1942 and 1944. On the morning of the tragically famous December 7, 1941, Japan attacked Pearl Harbor, inflicting extensive damage and causing a massacre among the military and civilian personnel of the small American outpost in the Pacific Ocean. The lack of a formal declaration of war by the Japanese country to the United States of America provoked, in the American public opinion, a sense of disapproval and hatred towards it, for what President Franklin Delano Roosevelt defined, in his speech to the nation, as the *Day of Infamy*. On December 11, 1941, four days after the Japanese attack on Pearl Harbor, Italy and Germany, faithful to the Tripartite Pact with Japan, declared war on the United States. Mussolini did so from the balcony of Piazza Venezia, while Hitler had a sober letter delivered to the American ambassador in Berlin. In it, the United States were reminded that they had repeatedly violated the state of non-belligerence between Washington and Berlin, and that several times the merchant ships had been seized by the U.S. Navy, which was believed to have, in addition, the order to fire on German military ships. For his part, Mussolini in his speech recalled that neither the German-Italian Axis nor Japan would have wished the extension of the conflict, directly accusing the American president Roosevelt of having pursued the war through a series of provocations.

These facts marked for the United States a fast armaments race, with the American war industry destined in a short time to a more than exponential growth in the production of weapons, warships and especially aircraft.

At the beginning of 1942, the American Air Force gradually increased its presence in the Mediterranean basin. In this area, until then, the balance of the conflict had always been in the balance between the Axis forces and the British and Commonwealth ones. The technological innovation and the firepower put in place by the U.S. war industry meant that quickly the fate of the Mediterranean conflict also changed radically in favor of the Allied powers. An unprecedented firepower was unleashed first on the cities of southern Italy and, during 1943, on the whole national territory, leading to the fall of the fascist regime, then to the armistice and later to the declaration of war by Italy to Germany itself. In little less than three years, the Allied military force had therefore succeeded in conquering a large part of the Italian territory, reaching the capital, Rome, on June 4, 1944.

The Author

THE AMERICANS IN THE MEDITERRANEAN

At the beginning of World War II, the Middle East theater of war represented an area at that time of exclusive British responsibility. The initial role of the then United States Army Air Corps (USAAC) was limited exclusively to the supply of arms and cooperation with their British counterparts through "reciprocal agreement". Army Air Corps observers did not arrive in Cairo until November 1940 to study Royal Air Force operations, crossed the Mediterranean, and observed the fighting on the Greek-Albanian front. Although the position of the United States of America at that time was neutral, U.S. President Franklin Delano Roosevelt's "Lend-Lease Act[1]" program provided the British and others with aircraft and armaments, as well as the instructors and supervisors needed to assemble, maintain, and overhaul U.S.-made aircraft and equipment. A delegation from the American airlines had also closely monitored the fighting in the Western Desert, which they described as a valuable test bed for their future aircraft designs. The North African battlefield also provided valuable information on aspects of anti-aircraft defense, from supply to communications and coordination between ground, air and naval forces. On June 21, 1941, USAAC was officially placed under a new centralized command known, as the United States Army Air Forces (USAAF), which included approximately 6,000 aircraft, 9,078 officers, and 143,563 soldiers. The following day Hitler invaded the Soviet Union. Despite the inability of the Wehrmacht to quickly defeat Joseph Stalin's Red Army, it still pushed deep into Russian territory. By November, the situation looked critical, with Crimea set to fall. The danger of a Soviet collapse would have had serious repercussions in the Middle East, with a possible German push to seize the substantial oil fields of Iran and Iraq. In conjunction with the Red Army's counterattack around Moscow, Japan made a surprise attack on the American port of Pearl Harbor on December 7, 1941, effectively forcing the United States to declare war on Japan. Three days later both Germany and Italy declared war on the United States as Allies of Japan. In Washington it was decided that the United States would fight jointly with the British against the three Axis powers (Germany, Italy and Japan). In early 1942, German U-boats indiscriminately sank merchant ships off the east coast of America and in the Caribbean. Allied fortunes were no better in the Far East, under the relentless Japanese advance.

The British lost Hong Kong (and soon it would be Singapore's turn), while and the United States struggled to hold the Philippines. In Europe, the Soviet Union was fighting a series of harsh winter offensives against German forces, now halted at the gates of Moscow. In North Africa, Field Marshall Erwin Rommel's 1942 surprise offensive brought a renewed threat to Egypt. The British Desert Air Force had been reinforced with the arrival of U.S. fighters and medium and heavy bombers originally intended for India, Australia, Russia, and the Far East. Washington decided to commit nine combat groups to North Africa, seven of which

---

1 The Lend-Lease Act was a legislative measure that allowed the United States to supply the United Kingdom, the Soviet Union, France, China, and other allied countries with large quantities of war materials without requiring immediate payment during World War II, between 1941 and 1945. In the previous period, in fact, exports of war materials from the United States were subject to the rules of the Neutrality Laws of 1937 and 1939, which required payment on delivery and transport on the buyer's merchant ship (the so-called "Cash & Carry"). The program began in March 1941, nine months before the attack on Pearl Harbor, and ended with the Surrender of Japan on September 2, 1945.

would be operational by the end of the year. In June 1942, twenty-three Consolidated B-24 Liberator bombers, under the command of Colonel Harry A. Halverson, were diverted to the Mediterranean after a stopover in Africa, originally destined for the 10th Air Force in China. On the night of June 11-12, thirteen of these "HALPRO" bombers took off from the RAF base at Fayd, Egypt, to launch an attack on Hitler's refineries in Romania, bombing the large complex at Ploieşti[2]. The raid, which marked the beginning of a concerted American presence in the Mediterranean, was also the first U.S. combat mission against German force in Europe. On 15 June, a joint attack followed with the RAF against the Italian naval force, which was sailing to intercept a convoy of Allied supplies bound for Malta, in what went down in history as Operation Vigorous. The overall outcome of the attack was the damage to the Italian battleship Littorio and the sinking of the cruiser *Trento*, in what is commonly remembered as the *Battle of Mid-June*[3].

On June 21, 1942, following the battle of Ain el-Gazala, the Axis Army reconquered the fortress of Tobruk. The new war scenario pushed with a certain urgency Roosevelt to transfer further armaments in the Middle East. Major General Lewis H. Brereton, commander of the 10th Air Force in India, received the order to send as many planes as possible to assist the British forces that were retreating in Egypt.

Nine Boeing B-17 Flying Fortress bombers were soon sent to the new war front. Brereton arrived in Cairo on June 25, 1942, along with 225 staff officers, pilots and mechanics. As Brereton worked to establish the 9th Air Force, three of the nine groups promised for the Middle East arrived: the 57th Fighter Group, equipped with Curtiss P-40s; the 12th Bombardment Group (Medium), with fifty-seven North American B-25 Mitchells; and the 98th Bombardment Group (Heavy) with its thirty-eight Consolidated B-24 Liberators. On June 28 the United States Army Middle East Air Force was activated under Brereton's leadership. Two days later his bombers began to strike Field Marshal Erwin Rommel's extensive supply lines. With the exception of the B-17 and B-24 Squadrons, Brereton's aircraft were assigned to the British Western Desert Air Force (WDAF), under the command of Air Vice Marshal Sir Arthur Coningham. On the evening of October 23, 1942, General Bernard L. Montgomery (commander of the British Eighth Army) launched an operation that went down in history as the Second Battle of El-Alamein. Preceded by a heavy four-hour artillery barrage, the ensuing battle was fought primarily on the ground with stubborn duels between German panzers and British tanks. Allied forces and medium bombers struck Italian-Ger-

---

2 HALPRO, or the Halverson Detachment, was a group of 23 Consolidated B-24 Liberators originally assigned to the 10th Air Force in the theater of operations in China, Burma and India. Under the command of Colonel Harry Halverson, the detachment was originally assigned to conduct raids on the Japanese National Islands. The detachment was to fly from Florida to China via Africa, but the Japanese offensive at Chekiang, China, in May 1942 interrupted this plan. This bomber force was then tasked with destroying German oil installations in support of the British in North Africa. HALPRO departed the United States on May 22, 1942, flying to Egypt via the Sudan. The 4,000-mile journey meant that some of the aircraft were grounded upon arrival in Egypt. On June 11, 1942, 13 HALPRO B-24s carried out the first USAAF attack in Europe, when they bombed oil refineries in Ploiesti, Romania; although the raid had little impact, it proved the concept that the heavy bomber could carry out long-range attacks against defended targets. The HALPRO detachment eventually remained in the Mediterranean theater. On 17 July 1942, the detachment was renamed Hal Bomb Squadron. It eventually formed the 376th Bombardment Group in October 1942.

3 The Battle of Mid-June refers to a series of air and sea battles that took place between 12 and 16 June 1942 in the central and eastern Mediterranean during World War II. The fighting, which is part of the wider Battle of the Mediterranean, saw the air and naval forces of Italy and Germany counter two supply operations on the island of Malta led by the British Royal Navy; with a clear success for the Axis forces.

man infantry positions, tanks and supply lines, while also maintaining constant pressure on Luftwaffe and Regia Aeronautica airfields. P-40s from the 57th Fighter Group shot down twenty-nine enemy aircraft while B-25 Mitchells helped disrupt two counterattacks. The crucial battle for Egypt was effectively over on November 4, 1942, with Rommel and the Axis troops in full retreat. The newly operational 9th Air Force USAAF began attacking targets in Libya and eastern Tunisia. American air power meanwhile continued to grow. By the end of 1942, 370 aircraft had arrived for the 9th Air Force, primarily P-40s, B-24 Liberators and B-25 Mitchells, as well as more than fifty Douglas C-47 Dakotas for transport.

▲ A railway station near the town of Cisterna di Latina.

FROM OPERATION TORCH TO THE FALL OF TUNISIA

As soon as he returned from his mission in Moscow, the British Prime Minister, Sir Winston Churchill, had started to press the Americans to speed up the preparations for the invasion of French North Africa.

On August 26, 1942, after a satisfactory meeting with the American commanders in Great Britain, the British Prime Minister had triumphantly telegraphed Roosevelt writing:

> «Henceforth I shall concentrate my thoughts on Torch [Operation] and you may rest assured that I shall do my best to see that your great strategic idea is crowned by the talks I have had with Eisenhower, Clark and our generals here in London; it seems to me that the best solution, indeed the only solution, to accomplish this consists in fixing the date for the start and subordinating everything to that date»[4].

Operation Torch, as agreed upon, would allow the conquest of Vichy's French North Africa by trapping Field Marshal Erwin Rommel between U.S. troops in the west and British troops in the east. The planning called for a series of amphibious landings under the command of Major General Dwight D. Eisenhower, involving primarily U.S. troops.

The operation would take place on November 8, 1942, on the Atlantic coast of Morocco, and on the Algerian coast near Algiers and Oran. This would have been the first major Allied invasion of the war against the Axis forces, and ultimately what would have resulted: the first major victory for the Allied coalition. In the early hours of November 8, 1942, three Allied task forces, commanded by Eisenhower, began their first combined assault against French Vichy positions across northwest Africa. The western task force, led by Major General George S. Patton with U.S. troops, landed at Casablanca (in west-central Morocco), initially encountering strong resistance. To the east, Major General Lloyd Fredendall's central task force approached Oran (in northwestern Algeria). After taking the port, the paratroopers captured the vital airfields of La Sénia and Tafaraoui. The Eastern Task Force, which consisted mainly of British troops under the command of Major General Charles Ryder, landed in Algiers and seized the important airfield of Maison Blanche. Eisenhower ordered British and American airborne units to also capture the Algerian airports at Bône and Youks-les-Bains, near the Tunisian border.

On November 9, the day after the invasion, German troops began arriving in Tunisia from Italy. By the end of the month, formations of Junkers Ju 52/3m transport planes had carried more than 15,000 men. By sea, heavy vehicles and another 2,000 men arrived in the main Tunisian ports of Bizerte and Tunis. On 14 November, General Walther Nehring quickly took command of the newly formed 5. Panzerarmee. The transfer of 155 aircraft to Tunisia increased the German force in North Africa, Sicily, and Sardinia, with nearly 700 combat aircraft by the end of December[5].

---

4 Roosevelt – Churchill, *Carteggio segreto di guerra*, Mondadori, Milano, 1977, p. 279.
5 Eduard Mark, Center for Air Force History, *Aerial Interdiction: Air Power and the Land Battle in Three American Wars*, Washington D.C.,1994, p. 24.

By the end of November, Allied ground forces under the command of Lieutenant General Kenneth Anderson were only sixteen miles west of the Tunisian capital.

On November 28, 1942, the two sides clashed. Experienced German formations, under the command of General Hans-Jurgen von Arnim, engaged with Eisenhower's troops in a hard fight, which forced the Americans to retreat about twenty miles to the west. In the meantime, on the air front, Luftwaffe and Regia Aeronautica aircraft from the Sardinian, Sicilian and Tunisian airports had strengthened their presence, giving the Allied air force a hard time. The sharp worsening of weather conditions in December 1942 reluctantly forced Eisenhower to put himself on the defensive line, relying on the air protection of Major General James H. Doolittle's 12th Air Force, activated on August 20, 1942.

These new air forces, once the North African bases were secured, completed the transfer of the units from the United Kingdom. The 12th Air Force would deploy over 1,000 combat aircraft to this new scenario, including: 400 P-39 Airacobra, P-40 and Spitfire short-range fighters, 240 P-38 Lightning long-range fighters, 70 B-17 Flying Fortress heavy bombers, 228 B-25 Mitchell and B-26 Marauder medium bombers, 72 A-20 Havoc, Douglas DB-7 light bombers and A-36A Invader fighter-bombers, plus 156 troop transport aircraft equipped to drop paratroopers.

The British Eastern Air Command, on the other hand, would be based at Algerian bases with a total of 454 aircraft, of which 234 fighters and 220 light, medium and reconnaissance bombers: a force equal to about one third of the American one.

The original plans for Operation Torch called for the appointment of an Allied Air Force commander general, although Eisenhower had spoken out against a coalition air force. As a result, throughout November and December 1942, U.S. and British pilots were engaged in separate battles, primarily in support of their respective ground forces. This approach, which proved ineffective, was not resolved until late 1942, when Eisenhower and his senior officers consolidated Allied air resources into a single organization, Mediterranean Air Command (MAC), under the command of Air Vice Marshall Arthur Tedder. Tedder was now able to direct the coalition's aircraft where he felt it was most needed.

On 4 December 1942, twenty Consolidated B-24 Liberators of the 98th Bombardment Group, 9th Air Force, attacked the port facilities of Naples. The large American four-engine aircraft, coming from the Kabrit and Fayid air bases in Egypt, were carrying large 1,000 and 2,000 lb demolition-type ordnance. For the American forces it was the first direct attack on the territory of an Axis nation; the incursion lasted only a few minutes, catching the population and the defenses of the port in the most complete surprise. The British had been bombing the major ports of southern Italy for years, but they did so mostly at night using Vickers Wellington bombers which also operated from Malta. The American pilots had spent more than 12 hours in the air in the action, which was defined as a great success and without any loss of aircraft. The port area was devastated, including the nearby houses; a cruiser of the Regia Marina moored inside the port perimeter was almost sunk. The war bulletin n. 924 issued on 5 December reported 159 dead and 358 wounded. Italy had just enough time to realize that the huge four-engine planes that had attacked Naples were American, when on the 11th of the same month a new formation of B-24s of the 98th and 376th Bombardment Group bombed the port of Naples. The formation with no fighter escort, led by Colonel

McGuire, dropped 35 1,000 lb bombs on the docks of the port of Naples. The Neapolitan city was not spared by the Liberators even on December 24, even though it was Christmas Eve; Taranto was also involved in this raid.

At the end of January 1943, with a new German offensive on North African soil, Eisenhower's troops faced a renewed test of strength. In January, the American air force focused its attention on the main ports of southern Italy, from where, among other things, the supplies for the Axis troops in North Africa departed. On January 7 Palermo was heavily bombed by B-24 Liberator. On the 11th it was again the turn of Naples, on which 40 bombs of 1,000 lbs rained down. This time the bombers suffered two heavy losses, including the aircraft of the formation leader, Lieutenant Colonel Payne. The shooting down of the two Liberators that crashed off the Gulf of Salerno was claimed by the pilots of the Macchi MC.202s of the 22nd C.T. Group of the Regia Aeronautica.

Another raid on the Neapolitan city followed on the 26th of the same month. During the night between 23 and 24 January, after having bombed Tripoli, Tunis and Crete, the B-24 Liberators of the 98th Bombardment Group returned to Sicily and attacked Palermo. The month, which ended with the attack on Messina by the large American four-engine aircraft, outlined a much broader picture of actions than the one in North Africa, making the cities and ports of southern Italy a favorite stop for American heavy bombers.

While on February 13 the bombers of the 9th Air Force attacked the airport of Crotone and various targets around the area of Naples, in North Africa from mid-February a second German push was underway; this time Rommel achieved an important victory against the American II Corps near the Kasserine Pass. Several days later, however, an Allied counter-attack reversed the German fortunes and helped seal the fate of the Axis in North Africa. Eisenhower was critical of hastily formed and trained U.S. air units. As an example of air incompetence he cited a bombing mission operated by B-17s against enemy troops at Kasserine Pass. The mission had proved to be a complete failure: the bombers had gotten lost en route and had dropped their bombs more than 100 miles from the target.

This episode also led to a new reorganization of the Allied air force, which resulted in the formation of the North African Air Force (NAAF), a component of the Allied Mediterranean Air Command (MAC), under the leadership of Lieutenant General Carl A. Spaatz. The ups and downs of the African Campaign pushed Eisenhower to undertake further internal reorganization, with the formation of the Northwest African Tactical Air Force (NATAF) under the leadership of Air Vice Marshal Sir Arthur Coningham, and the Northwest African Strategic Air Force (NASAF) under the leadership of Major General James H. Doolittle, the hero of Tokyo. Allied tactical aviation was immediately transformed by introducing Coningham's philosophy of first destroying the Luftwaffe and only then isolating the battlefield, a doctrine well proven in combat, and used by the British both at El-Alamein and later in the pursuit of Rommel across the desert. To Eisenhower and senior Allied officers assembled on February 16, 1943, Coningham had stressed that "the Army has one battle to fight, the ground battle. The Air [Force] has two. It must first beat the enemy in the air: that it may enter the ground battle against the enemy ground forces with as much power as possible!" Improved weather in March 1943 allowed the growing number of Allied aircraft to go airborne, hitting strategic and tactical targets.

Since the beginning of the conflict, in addition to the ports (now constantly targeted), the airports of Sardinia and western Sicily, due to their geographical position, had offered the fastest and safest way to reach the coasts of North Africa. On February 17, more than 40 B-17 Flying Fortresses attacked the Sardinian airport of Elmas, with B-25 Mitchells and B-26 Marauders destined for those of Villacidro and Decimomannu. The next day the bombing was repeated and also involved Elmas and Cagliari.

The B-17 Flying Fortress of the 301st Bombardment Group of NASAF bombed Sicily on March 22, bombing Palermo with 72 tons of bombs. The damages were huge and the victims amounted to 38 dead and 184 wounded.

On March 24, the B-24s of the IX Bomber Command bombed Messina between 14:00 and 17:00 hours. The nineteen B-24 Liberators of the 98th Bombardment Group, led by Captain J. R. Muehlberg, dropped 55 tons of ordnance on the port.

In addition to the maritime merchant traffic, which was by now unable to move in the central Mediterranean, both the Regia Aeronautica (with its large transport aircraft including the Fiat G.12 and the Savoia-Marchetti SM.82 of the Servizi Aerei Speciali (SAS)) and the Luftwaffe (with the Junkers Ju52/3m and the Messerschmitt Me 323 Gigant) guaranteed support to the Italian-German troops on the North African front. At the airports of Castelvetrano, Trapani Milo, and Trapani Chinisia, the so-called Gigants, the largest transport planes of the Luftwaffe, capable of carrying up to 130 passengers, continuously stopped. According to estimates made by the Allies, 8 Messerschmitt Me 323 made one trip per day to Tunisia, carrying up to 455 tons of war material, for a weekly total of about 3,200 tons. It is estimated that at least 40,000 tons of supplies were needed per month to support the Italian-German forces in Tunisia.

The airport of Castelvetrano was one of the main airports: in the period from February 26th to March 7th, there were 54 flights of Ju 52/3m from Castelvetrano to various airports in Tunisia; of these, the Allied Intelligence Section ascertained that 23 were carrying fuel and the remaining 31 ammunition for the Afrikakorps. The B-17 bombers of the NASAF attacked the airports of Castelvetrano and Trapano Milo on April 13.

On April 16 a heavy raid hit the city of Etna. The one carried out by the B-24 Liberator on Catania was a real massacre among the civilians; the bombs hit in full the city center, causing the death of 146 people and the wounding of 291, with very serious damages to the city. Other heavy attacks were repeated on the same targets on 17 and 18 April.

On April 26, twenty-seven B-17s of the 97th Bombardment Group bombed the Grosseto airport, while a massive formation of seventy B-24 Liberators attacked the Bari airport with 20 and 500 lb. ordnance. The bombing of Grosseto, which took place on Easter Monday, remained impressed on Italian public opinion, not so much for the bombs dropped on the military structures of the airport, but for those that hit the amusement park on a festive day. The martyrdom of the children of Grosseto was exploited by fascist propaganda, defining it as Allied barbarism. On April 29 "La Stampa" wrote about the "savage raid" that "the dead among the civilian population of Grosseto following the recent enemy raid had risen as a result of further investigations to 145 and the wounded to 268, of which 100 with minor injuries. The victims, for the most part women and children, were machine-gunned at an almost level flight in the center and in the streets of the town..."

OBJECTIVE: SICILY

Between January 14 and 24, 1943, an inter-allied conference was held in Casablanca, Morocco, during which the British and American political and military leaders, led by Churchill and Roosevelt, had agreed on the plan of future operations. The American General Staff had pushed for a landing in France, to launch a direct attack on Germany; the British, however, considered the presence of German troops on French territory too strong and feared a defeat.

The strategic objectives were the complete dominion of the Mediterranean, the exit from the war of Italy and the immobilization of considerable German forces, some of which would have come from France. At the end of the long debate it was decided that the first step in Europe would be taken in Sicily.

When the remaining Axis forces in Tunisia surrendered on May 13, 1943, the Allied powers prepared to attack the "soft underbelly of Fortress Europe", following the vivid expression of the British Prime Minister, Sir Winston Churchill.

Churchill, who had come out victorious in the Battle of Britain, certainly did not like the words expressed by the Italian press of the regime regarding the bombing carried out by the Luftwaffe on the English city of Coventry on November 14, 1940, and on April 8 and 10, 1941, which caused the death of 1,236 innocent people.

The British idea was to strike the enemy's resources wherever they were. The risk, otherwise, was that those same resources would have been used against them.

The two islands of Lampedusa and Pantelleria are the farthest Italian outposts, closest to Africa and sentinels of Italy. For this reason, it was mandatory to conquer them before any other.

All Allied air power was therefore focused on the smaller islands of Sicily. Thus began the preparatory phase of Operation Corkscrew, which culminated with the occupation of the island of Pantelleria.

Already on May 9, in the preparatory phase, General Eisenhower had decided to employ on Sicily the heavy bombers of NASAF (Northwest African Strategic Air Force) and the fighters and fighter-bombers of NATAF (Northwest African Tactical Air Force). The Royal Air Force in Malta was to provide indirect support to the operations by escorting the bombers bound to attack the Sicilian air bases. The commander of the strategic air forces in the Mediterranean, General James H. Doolittle, who had become very popular for his daring air raid on Tokyo in April 1942, completed his preparations by deploying most of the available air forces in the area of Constantine, Souk-El-Arba and Djedeida.

The commander of the tactical air force, Air Vice Marshal Arthur Coningham, had instead moved medium and light bombers to the ground on the Cape Bon peninsula. In total, at the beginning of operations against Pantelleria, NATAF and NASAF together deployed 1,017 aircraft in full combat efficiency, supported by a fair number of reserve aircraft. Due to the reduced range of the numerous single-engine tactical support aircraft, the XII Air Support Command (ASC), hierarchically subordinate to NATAF, decentralized its units between May 20 and June 4 on the fields of the Capo Bon peninsula closest to the area of operations.

In addition to the above mentioned attack force, the operation was indirectly supported by a group of air units, including the bombers of the Middle East and the Coastal Air Command, which reached a total of 3,395 aircraft. To conquer the island of Pantelleria, Eisenhower chose the British 1st Infantry Division, which had received training in amphibious warfare in England, but had not been selected for the invasion of Sicily.

The first week of May marked the final Allied rush of the African Campaign. On the 1st, 4th and 6th the B-24 Liberators attacked Reggio Calabria, and on the 4th also Taranto.

Paradoxically, on Wednesday, May 5, Benito Mussolini had announced, during what would be the last speech of his life delivered from the balcony of Palazzo Venezia, the "supreme certainty of victory" as reported in the title of an article appeared in those days in the "Corriere della Sera". In what will be the last speech of his life.

On May 9, Palermo was put to fire and sword by a wave of intense and non-stop bombing raids: during the day, a total of 122 B-17 Flying Fortresses, 89 B-25 Mitchell and B-26 Marauders and, during the night, 23 Vickers Wellingtons of the RAF, had unloaded a total of 485 tons of bombs on the Sicilian capital.

At dawn on the 11th, the 9th Air Force USAAF sent from various airports in Libya 48 B-24 Liberator heavy bombers, 26 of the 98th and 22 of the 376th Bombardment Group, with a large escort of 47 RAF Spitfires coming from Malta. The main target of the bombardment was the port of Catania, where the bombers unloaded in several waves from an altitude between 22,000 and 25,000 feet (depending on the position inside the combat box), 230 500 lb bombs, and 60 4 lb incendiary bombs, for a total of 113 tons of ordnance. The devastating bombardment killed 216 people and wounded 303, mostly civilians. On Friday, 14 May, 46 B-17 Flying Fortresses of the 2nd and 99th Bombardment Groups flew into Civitavecchia, north of Rome, destroying several boats, while 36 B-26 Marauders of the 320th Bombardment Group attacked Porto Ponte Romano in Sardinia.

On May 20 the Flying Fortresses reached Grosseto, bombing the airport. On the 21st, a formation of 21 B-24 Liberators from the 376th Bombardment Group attacked Villa San Giovanni and another 24 B-24s from the 98th Bombardment Group headed for Reggio Calabria. Incursions were made over most of southern Italy and Sardinia. In Sicily, a violent wave of bombing involved the airfields of Castelvetrano and Sciacca, in which just under 100 B-17s participated.

On the 28th, while the 9th Air Force bombed in two separate missions the airport complex of Foggia and the port of Augusta, in Sicily, the 93 Flying Fortresses of the 2nd, 97th, 99th and 301st Bombardment Group reached in the middle of the day the port of Livorno, where they dropped more than 1.000 500 lb. bombs.

The month ended with the bombing of the Foggia airport complex by 96 B-17s of the 5th Bomb Wing.

On June 1 Pantelleria was attacked by 19 B-17 Flying Fortresses of the 97th Bombardment Group USAAF, escorted by 28 P-38 Lightning of the 82nd FG, 12 of which armed with a 1,000 lb bomb.

June 11 marked the fall of the island of Pantelleria; NATAF had carried out a total of 728 sorties in 63 missions against it, and 154 sorties in 14 missions against Lampedusa. In all, almost 1,100 aircraft had participated in the final assault, dropping 1,571 tons of bombs, for a total, for the period from 1st to 10th June, of 4,844 tons of ordnance, distributed in 3,647 sorties. From the 8th of May to the 11th of June, Pantelleria suffered from the NAAF a total of 5.285 effective sorties, at the expense, for the Allied forces, of 16 damaged aircrafts and 14 lost in action, for a total of 6.200 tons of bombs launched.

AIR FORCE ASSIGNED TO USAAF GROUPS	
Heavy bombers	48 aircrafts in 4 Squadrons of 12 aircrafts
Medium Bombers	57 aircraft in 4 Squadrons of 13 aircraft, plus 5 from Headquarters
Light Bombers	57 aircraft in 4 Squadrons of 13 aircraft, plus 5 from Headquarters
Fighter Bombers	57 aircraft in 4 Squadrons of 13 aircraft, plus 5 from Headquarters
Hunters	75 aircrafts in 3 Squadrons of 25 aircrafts
Troop transport	52 aircrafts in 4 Squadrons of 13 aircrafts

Northwest African Air Forces
Lieutenant General Carl Spaatz
June 1, 1943

Northwest African Strategic Air Force (NASAF)
Major General James Doolittle
USAAF 2nd, 97th, 99th, & 301st Bombardment Groups (B-17)
USAAF 310th & 321st Bombardment Groups (B-25)
USAAF 17th, 319th, & 320th Bombardment Groups (B-26)
USAAF 1st, 14th, & 82nd Fighter Groups (P-38)
USAAF 325th Fighter Group (P-40)
RAF 4 Wings (Wellington)

Northwest African Tactical Air Force (NATAF)
Acting Air Marshal Sir Arthur Coningham

Tactical Bomber Force
Air Commodore Laurence Sinclair
USAAF 47th Bombardment Group (A-20)
*USAAF 12th & 340th Bombardment Groups (B-25)
RAF 2 Tactical Reconnaissance Squadrons
RAF 2 Wings
SAAF 1 Wing

XII Air Support Command
Major General Edwin House
USAAF 33rd & *324th Fighter Groups (P-40)
USAAF 31st Fighter Group (Spitfire)
USAAF 27th & 86th Fighter Groups (A-36)
USAAF 111th Observation Squadron

Western Desert Air Force
Air Vice-Marshal Harry Broadhurst
*USAAF 57th & 79th Fighter Groups (P-40)
RAF Fighter Wings (Spitfire)
SAAF Fighter Wing (Spitfire)

*9th Air Force Groups

Northwest African Coastal Air Force (NACAF)
Air Vice-Marshal Sir Hugh Lloyd
USAAF 81st & 350th Fighter Groups (P-39)
USAAF 52nd Fighter Group (Spitfire)
RAF 3 Wings & Other Units
RN Fleet Air Arm Squadrons
Two Air Defense Commands
USAAF 1st & 2nd Antisubmarine Squadrons

Northwest African Troop Carrier Command (NATCC)
Brigadier General Paul Williams
USAAF 51st Wing (C-47)
60th, 62nd, & 64th Groups
USAAF 62nd Wing (C-47)
61st, 313th, 314th, & *316th Groups
RAF No. 38 Wing

Northwest African Training Command (NATC)
Brigadier General John Cannon
Three replacement battalions
USAAF 68th Observation Group
Miscellaneous training units

Northwest African Air Service Command (NAASC)
Major General Delmar Dunton

Northwest African Photographic Reconnaissance Wing (NAPRW)
Colonel Elliott Roosevelt
USAAF 3rd Photographic Group
SAAF No. 60 Squadron
RAF No. 682 Squadron
French 2/33 Squadron

▲ Consolidate B-24 Liberator s/n 41-11593 "Black Maria II," one of 23 B-24s in the original HALPRO formation. Passed to the 376th Bombardment Group, it was assigned Radio Call Letter (RCL) #18. Piloted by Lieutenant Colonel John H. Payne, it participated in the first HALPRO mission on 12 June 1942 over the oil refineries at Ploiesti, Romania. It operated missions over Tobruk, Benghazi, Crete and took part in the second HALPRO mission against the Italian fleet on 15 June 1942.

▼ The B-24D s/n 41-11591 "Lorraine" RCL #45, belonging to the 513th Bombardment Squadron, 376th Bombardment Group. Also from the original formation of HALPRO. Piloted by Major Norman Appold, it participated in the first American raid over Naples on 4 December 1942, and in the Palermo raid on 7 January 1943. The last mission over Italy was carried out on September 16, 1943 over Potenza.

▲ Gunners clip bombs onto the wings of a Curtiss P-40K of the 9th Air Force, North Africa. The aircraft belongs to the 64th Fighter Squadron, of the 57th Fighter Group. Note the desert coloring and the Scorpion identifying the Squadron.

▼ General James Harold Doolittle, known as Jimmy. He was the creator and leader of the air formation in the raid on Tokyo, which occurred on April 18, 1942, and went down in history as the Doolittle raid. This was the first air attack that the United States of America conducted on Japanese soil during World War II. The USAAF's sixteen North American B-25 Mitchell bombers took off from the deck of the United States Navy's aircraft carrier USS Hornet. The bombing was organized as a response to the Japanese attack on Pearl Harbor on December 7, 1941, and had more of a moral value than a tactical or strategic one.

▲ Photo of the bombing of the port of Naples on 11 December 1942 by the Consolidated B-24 Liberator of the 9th Air Force. On that occasion one of the bombers belonging to the 98th BG was shot down by anti-aircraft fire.

▼ The German Dornier Do 17Z 3U+FU bomber of Zerstörergeschwader 26 (ZG26), found by the Americans on 26 January 1943 at Castel Benito airfield, Libya.

▲ Consolidate B-24D Liberator s/n 42-40654 "Kate Smith" belonging to the 345th Bombardment Squadron, 98th Bombardment Group, under repair after an off-field landing.

▼ Bombing of the port and railway station of Messina. The first American bombing of the city happened on January 26 th 1943 to work of the bombers B-24 Liberator of the 9th Air Force. 17 August 1943 the city was conquered by the Allied troops, decreeing the end of the campaign of Sicily.

▲ Mechanics at work on one of four Wright R-1820-97 "Cyclone" turbocharged radial engines, of the Boeing B-17F Flying Fortress s/n 42-5346 "The Reluctant Dragon", here belonging to the 97th BG, probably at Chateaudun-du-Rhumel, Algeria.

▼ Bombs dropped on the city of Palermo in the attack of March 22, 1943, by 24 B-17s of the 301st Bombardment Group. It was the first bombing by the Northwest African Strategic Air Force (NASAF) on the island.

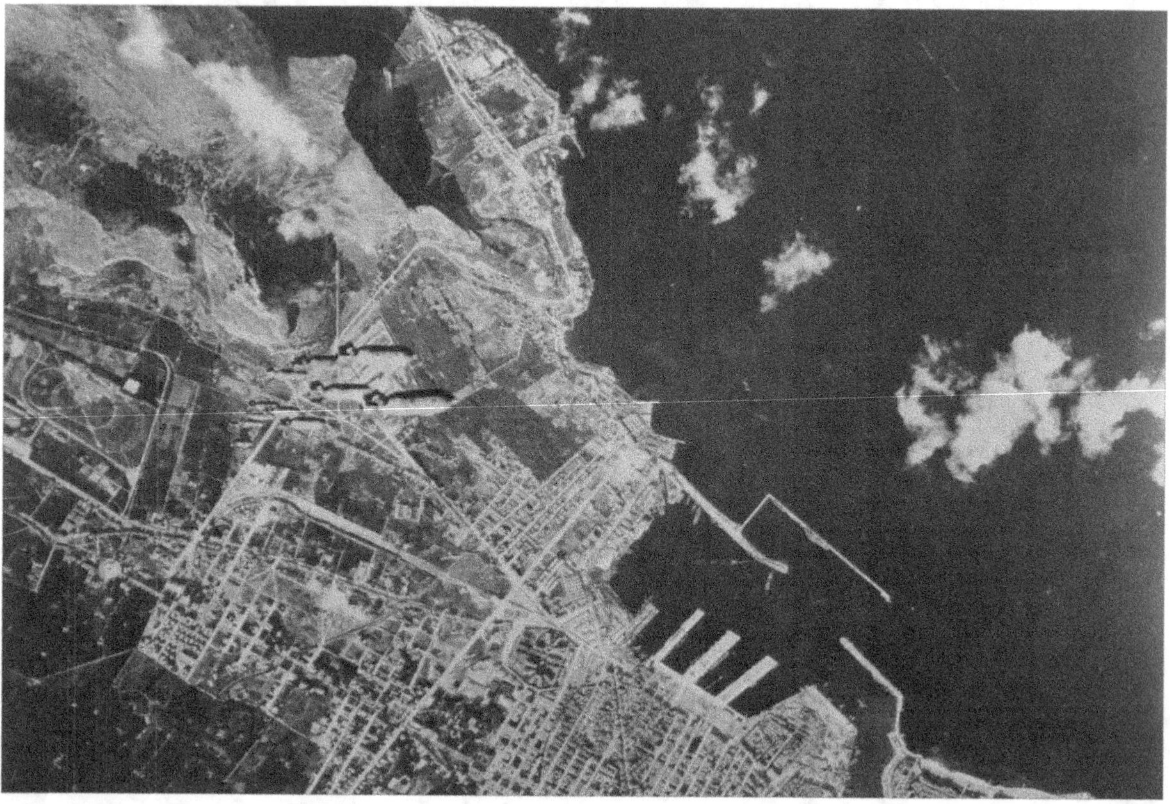

▲ The church of San Pietro in Piazza Castello, Palermo, destroyed by Allied bombing.

▲ Air Vice-Marshal Sir Arthur Tedder, commander in chief of Mediterranean Air Command (left) lights a cigarette to Major General Carl Spaatz, commander of the Northwest African Air Forces (NAAF). Behind them is a map of the theater of operations in the central Mediterranean.

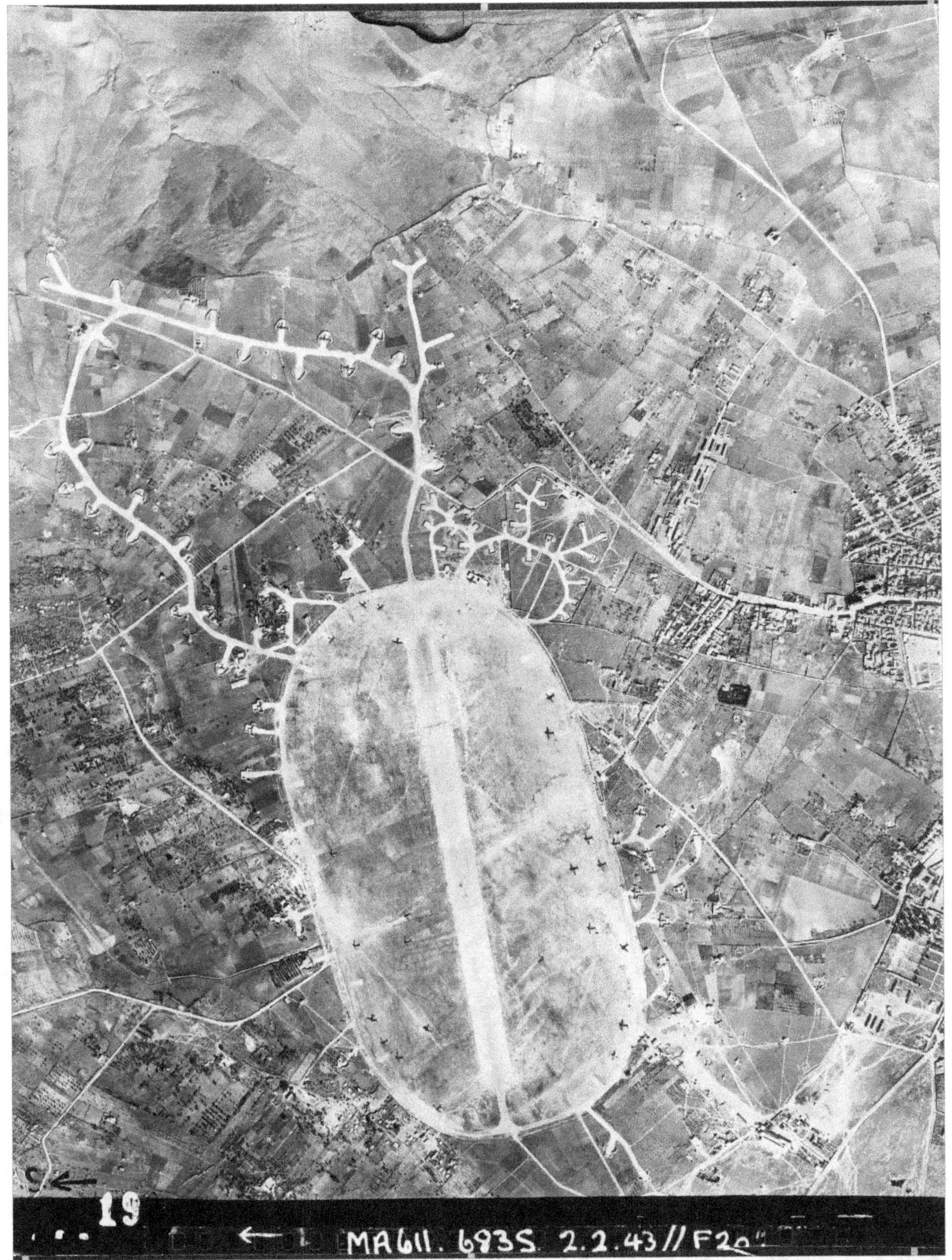

▲ Aerial photo of Castelvetrano aerodrome, taken on February 2, 1943 from a Spitfire PR of 683 Squadron RAF. The silhouettes of many large transport aircraft are clearly visible on the airport. The first NASAF B-17s bombed the airport only on April 13, 1943, during Operation Flax.

▲ In the foreground, a large 2,000-pound device is rolled by two servicemen. In the background is the B-24D s/n 41-11636 "Wash's Tub," also one of HALPRO's bombers. Initially transferred to the 98th Bombardment Group, it was later assigned to the 376th Bombardment Group. It took part in the low-level mission over the refineries in Ploiesti, Romania. During its 15 months in the Middle East, it flew 73 missions, dropping 219 tons of bombs, flying 551 hours and 100,000 miles in wartime scenarios and shooting down 22 enemy fighter planes.

▼ From left: Major General Carl Spaatz, Colonel Elliot Roosevelt and General Alexander, along with other officers, analyze photos taken by Allied aerial reconnaissance ahead of new operations. Colonel Elliot Roosevelt, son of the president of the United States of America, was head of the Northwest African Photographic Reconnaissance Wing (NAPRW).

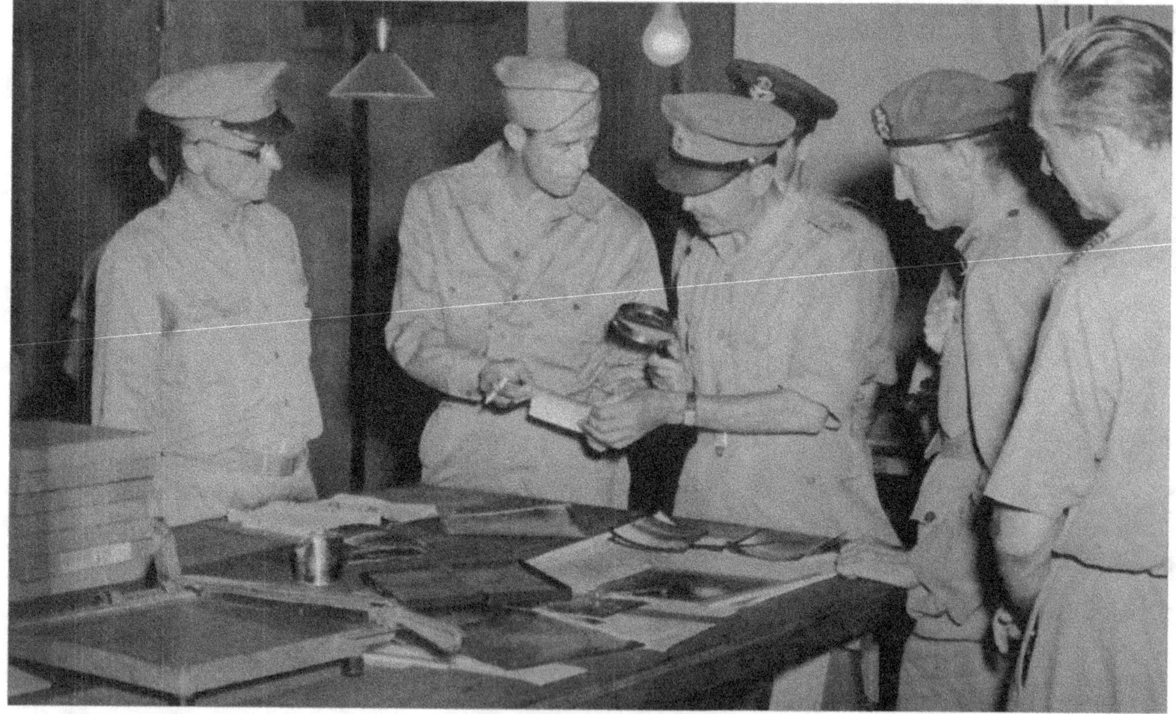

▲ Picture of the bombing of Augusta (SR), which took place on May 13, 1943 by 28 B-24 Liberators of the 376th Bombardment Group, led on that occasion by Colonel Keith K. Compton himself. Note on the right the numerous seaplanes at the buoy. An initial death toll from the air raid was 19 dead and 41 wounded.

▼ The bombing of the city of Cagliari on May 13, 1943. Here the attack carried out by B-17s of the 414th BS, 97th BG. An initial casualty toll was 10 dead and 56 wounded, as reported in Bulletin No. 1,084 of May 14, 1943.

▲ Some buildings destroyed by the Allied bombardment of Cagliari. On the 13th of May 1943 the 12th Air Force attacked with particular intensity the seaplane base and the port of Cagliari. On that day, a force of 96 B-25s and 107 B-17s dropped over 400 tons of ordnance on the city.

▼ The bombing of Alghero Airport, Sardinia, by NASAF Martin B-26 Marauders on May 24, 1943. Note the many aircraft in the off-center areas.

▲ Bombing of Grottaglie airfield on June 4, 1943, by 46 B-24 Liberators of the 98th and 376th BG.

▼ Comiso airport, bombed at 13:22 on 17 June 1943 by 23 B-24s of the 376th BG. The American four-engine aircraft dropped about 62 tons of explosive devices on it. The damage to the airport structures was considerable, with 4 Messerschmitt Bf 109 fighters destroyed and 3 seriously damaged, all belonging to the Luftwaffe Jagdgeschwader 53 "Pik As".

▲ The Martin B-26B Marauder s/n 41-17724 "Rabbit/ Red Hot" piloted by 1st Lieutenant John B. Stumm of the 444th BS, 320th BG. On 15 June 1943 it was seriously damaged by Flak after bombing the airport of Trapani Milo, Sicily; it was therefore forced to make an emergency landing in North Africa.

▼ Bombing of Gerbini airport on June 13, 1943. The mission was carried out by 24 B-24 of the 376th BG, which dropped almost 55 tons of bombs on the runway. While returning, the formation was intercepted by Axis fighters who inflicted two losses.

▲ A Fairchild K-20 type camera. It was one of the lightest and most maneuverable aerial cameras issued to the U.S. Air Force during World War II, and was particularly well suited for taking rapid oblique images.

▲ The city of Catania bombed on July 11, 1943. During the day 73 B-17 of the NASAF unloaded almost 200 tons of 500 pound bombs. The raid caused 28 dead and 75 wounded.

▼ The crew of B-17F s/n 41-24346 "Avenger", belonging to the 419th BS, 301st BG. Here they are interrogated after the raid on Naples on April 4, 1943. The bomber then switched to the 348th BS, 99th BG and operated from the base at Tortorella, Italy.

▲ S/Sgt. Benjamin F. Warmer, of San Francisco, Calif. He holds a Browning M2 machine gun, in his position as Waist gunner on a B-17F of the 99th BG. Warmer starred in the air raid on Gerbini on July 5, 1943, when he single-handedly managed to shoot down seven Axis aircraft.

▲ Paratroopers from the 505th Parachute Infantry Regiment, 82nd Airborne Division embark on the Douglas C-47-DL s/n 41-18341 "Lady from Hades" of the 61st Troop Carrier Squadron, 64th Troop Carrier Group. American paratroopers will play an important part, first in Sicily on July 10, 1943 in Operation Husky, and later in southern Italy with Operation Avalanche.

▼ Three pilots of the 1st Fighter Group, pictured here in North Africa in front of Lockheed P-38G Lightning s/n 42-13010. From left to right: 2nd Lieutenant Howard A. Gilliam (MIA), 1st Lieutenant Leonard P. Stephan, 2nd Lieutenant Harold C. Lentz. Gilliam was shot down near Caltagirone (CT) on 10 July 1943 by the Flak of the German division Hermann Göring.

THE INVASION OF ITALY

The offensive plan for Operation Husky had been drawn up by General Harold Alexander the previous May 2, during a conference called by General Eisenhower in Algiers. There were to be two landing zones. The area of competence of the Seventh American Army, under the command of General George Patton, would have gone from Licata to Scoglitti, for a length of about eighty kilometers. Initially, three Divisions and other minor units would have landed, preceded by the launching of paratroopers that would have had to take possession of some key defensive positions. The area of competence of the British Eighth Army, commanded by General Bernard L. Montgomery, would have been the one that from the Gulf of Noto extended to Punta Castelluzzo (west of Capo Passero) for more than 50 kilometers; in this area would have landed four Infantry Divisions, two Armored Brigades and other minor units.

On July 2, 91 B-24 Liberators bombed the airfields of Lecce, Grottaglie and San Pancrazio Salentino, losing 4 bombers; B-25 Mitchells bombed the airfield of Sciacca, while P-40s engaged in high-altitude fights with hunters of the Regia Aeronautica and the Luftwaffe. Between May 14 and July 3, the Luftwaffe increased the number of its aircraft in the Mediterranean theater from 820 to 1,280. But the strength of squadrons based in Sicily and southern Italy rose only from 615 to 635; most of the reinforcements went to Sardinia, Greece and northern Italy. On July 5, the air force in Northwest Africa had, in contrast, 4,920 aircraft (excluding gliders). Approximately 2,900 of these were fighters and bombers[6]. The destructive force of the NAAF's bombers had been able to destroy anything at the island's airports and dirt runways. On July 5, Allied air forces had clashed with a massive formation of about 100 Italian-German fighters in the Gerbini area. Three B-17s were lost in action; they belonged to the first formation of the 99th Bombardment Group, which nevertheless managed to drop 3,240 fragmentation bombs, destroying some 28 fighter planes on the ground. In the course of the day other formations alternated in successive waves on the same targets. All the air forces of the Luftwaffe (with Jagdgeschwader 53 and 77), and the Regia Aeronautica (especially with the men of the 4th C.T. Wing of the Cavallino Rampante) had put up a tenacious resistance, paying a high price in terms of lives and equipment.

After the Allied landing, and the initial clashes in the area of Gela with the German Armored Division Hermann Göring and the Livorno Infantry Division, within a short time the Anglo-American positions on the bridgeheads were consolidated, and the Italian-German air force, after some initial attempts, proved unable to seriously interfere with the Allied ground advance.

On July 12, after rejecting the counterattack by the German Schmalz Group and the Italian Naples Division, the British XIII Corps of General Sir Miles Christopher Dempsey conquered Augusta, which together with Syracuse represented a maritime square of great operational importance for Eisenhower, since these ports were to serve as a logistical base for the landing of numerous vehicles and troops that would have given life to the ongoing operations on the eastern side of the island.

---

6 Eduard Mark, *op. cit.*, p. 58.

On July 14th, the fast advance of the ground troops in Sicily had allowed the conquest of six airports, which were quickly put in condition to operate. One week after the landing, eighteen and a half NAAF Squadrons, of which seven and a half belonged to the USAAF, were already operating from the airstrips of Pachino, Comiso, Biscari Santo Pietro (Caltagirone), Gela Ponte Olivo, Gela Farello and Licata.

On the same day the B-17, B-25 and B-26s appeared over Messina, Enna, Marsala and Randazzo, with the A-36A Invader and P-38 Lightning attacking numerous targets of opportunity on the island. However, a much broader strategic objective had been defined, and it was to interrupt the flow of supplies for the Italian-German troops through the railway stations and ports of southern Italy, focusing on those of Naples, Villa San Giovanni and Messina. On July 15 a formation of B-24s attacked Villa San Giovanni, seriously damaging the infrastructure and destroying most of the tracks. In the afternoon of the same day 72 B-17s of the 5th Bombardment Wing attacked Naples losing one B-17.

To prevent the arrival of additional German-Italian air forces from other bases in Italy or from Europe, the bombers increased the pressure on the airports in central Italy. The B-24 Liberators of the 9th Air Force from bases in Cyrenaica bombed the airports of Foggia on the 15th and Bari on the 16th, losing three B-24s; the B-25s and B-26s of the NASAF hit the airport of Vibo Valentia. The town of Randazzo, on the slopes of Etna, was hit on the 15th by the A-20 Boston and B-25 of the NATAF.

Thus, as the first week of the Sicilian campaign drew to a close, Allied ground forces had occupied about a third of the island, and the forces had effectively neutralized air resistance. During this period, the Northwest African Tactical Air Force (NATAF) flew 7,036 fighter and fighter-bomber missions and 768 bomber sorties, 510 of which were against enemy positions and supply lines. The Strategic Wing carried out 1,720 sorties with bombers, of which 1,031 were against positions and lines of communication and 827 sorties flown by fighter aircraft. Northwest African Coastal Air Force aircraft were also intensively employed on 1,562 sorties, four-fifths of which were convoy escorts. The total for all elements was 12,715 sorties. The weight of the bombs dropped reached 4,530 tons.

At 14:30 on July 17, seventy-seven B-24 Liberators of the 9th Air Force hit the Naples railroad yard. About an hour later, 49 B-17s of the NASAF arrived at the same targets; at 4 p.m. on the dot 107 B-26 Marauders escorted by 98 P-38s arrived. Finally, another 48 B-17s and 72 B-25s, escorted by 67 P-38s, attacked various targets around Naples. Although the Americans left some B-26s and a B-24 on the field, in all they dropped about 868 tons of bombs in what was the largest American air raid of the summer.

In the summer of 1943, the scruples that had restrained British Prime Minister Churchill and his Foreign Minister Eden from bombing the city of Rome had failed, and the Allies decided to launch a large-scale punitive and demonstrative action[7]. Already Eisenhower, at the time of the invasion of Sicily, had made it clear that they were landing on a land rich in historical and architectural evidence, but had also added that no monument was worth the life of a single soldier.

On 19 July the first bombardment of Rome was carried out, which began at 11:03 and ended at 13:35, and occurred in two phases: the first, from 11:03 to 12:10, over the Littorio and

---

7 Anthony Eden served as British Foreign Secretary for several terms, and then became Prime Minister from 1955 to 1957.

San Lorenzo railway stations as primary targets; the second from 12:12 to 13:35 over the Littorio and Ciampino airports. The formations of the four-engined B-17 Flying Fortress and B-24 Liberator, and of the twin-engined B-25 Mitchell and B-26 Marauder of the 9th and 12th Air Force, arrived in Rome from two directions: from the north-west, entering from the sea between Civitavecchia and Ladispoli, turning right towards the city, and from Nettuno, penetrating the coast south of the city and continuing straight towards Ciampino. By doing so, the work of the spotters was favored and they found themselves all targets lined up on the same slightly transversal axis: the Littorio area on the Salaria, the Tiburtino-San Lorenzo district, the Ciampino airport area on the Appia.

Over Rome, in the late morning, four groups of B-17 Flying Fortresses of the 5th Bombardment Wing of the NASAF, and groups of B-24 Liberators of the 9th Air Force took turns; in all 156 B-17 Flying Fortresses of the 12th and 117 B-24 Liberators of the 9th Air Force took off from Tunisia, Algeria and Libya. The 273 four-engine aircraft pounded the railway junction on the Salaria and the San Lorenzo station for an hour and twenty minutes; a Squadron of Flying Fortresses of the 99th Bombardment Group also targeted the Tiburtino airport, at Portonaccio.

Shortly before noon, 117 B-26 Marauders and 144 B-25 Mitchell medium twin-engine bombers also arrived and attacked Littorio and Ciampino airports. Together, the 12th Air Force bombers constituted a substantial air fleet, the most powerful ever assembled over a single city in Italy. Escorting the bombers were twin-tailed P-38 Lightning fighters, which, in the interval between waves, descended to low altitudes to strafe mainly the large squares, such as Piazzale del Verano, Largo Preneste and Piazzale Prenestino.

In little more than two hours of apocalypse, 1,060 tons of explosives were dropped on Rome, something like 4,000 bombs and incendiary fragments: it was the largest incursion carried out until that moment on Italy, also in terms of launched tonnage[8].

Carl Spaatz, head of the NAAF, affirmed that "the mission of 19 July over Rome had been a monument to the precision of the American method of bombing[9]", adding that "it had been very difficult to achieve the objectives of the mission". He added that "it had been very uninteresting from the point of view of the air force because it had been too easy[10]".

In the meantime in Sicily the front line had moved around the volcano Etna, where the Italian-German forces had placed on the heights the artillery of the XIV Panzerkorps. The fight in the area of Catania was hard, with the Eighth Army of Montgomery in serious difficulty in the area of the Simeto river a few steps from Catania. The persistence of the stalemate situation led "the fox of the desert" to aim with his Divisions towards the hinterland, leaving for the moment stranded the possibility to conquer the city of Etna in a short time. The main centers of communication that formed a circle around Etna, among which the most important were Catania, Randazzo, Troina, Adrano, Acireale and Fiumefreddo, became the new objectives of the aircraft of the NATAF; to them were added on the Tyrrhenian side also Barcellona Pozzo di Gotto and Milazzo. Milazzo was bombed on the 25th of July by B-25 Mitchells and P-40s.

---

8 The tragic record will be set less than a month later in Milan, where on the night of August 13 the Lancasters and Halifax of the RAF will drop 1,904 tons of bombs and another 1,534 tons two nights later.
9 The History of the Twelfth Air Force, Pantelleria, Sicily, p. 120 (AFHRA A-6202).
10 Craven Wesley Frank e Cate James Lea, *The Army Air Force in World War II*, The University of Chicago Press, 1949, p. 463.

During the evening of July 22, the American Seventh Army entered in Palermo. The conquest of the Sicilian capital marked a clear change of pace in the battle of Sicily. Upon Montgomery's invitation, Patton reached Syracuse by plane, to discuss the common strategy to be adopted, in view of the final phase of the operations in Sicily. Patton had already established that in order to reach Messina, his Army would have to follow two roads, both north of Etna: the coastal SS113, which went from Palermo to Messina, and the SS120, a mountain road, very treacherous, which passed inland and crossed Sicily from Nicosia to Randazzo.

On July 30, the troops of the First Canadian Division conquered Catenanuova, in the hinterland of Enna. The first of August the Americans made their entrance in Santo Stefano di Camastra, with the British troops that captured the important airport of Gerbini, a few kilometers from Catania.

From July 10 to August 5, Catania itself suffered numerous attacks by 39 heavy bombers, 172 medium, 10 light bombers and 309 fighter-bombers.

In order to conquer the positions on Troina and Adrano, both key places of the Etna line, the Tactical Air Force played a direct and important role. From July 8 to August 6, 265 fighter-bombers, 97 light bombers and 12 medium bombers went against Troina. They inflicted such severe damage that, according to an officer of the ground forces, thirty-six hours were necessary for the engineers to open a passage through the rubble of the city. From July 10 to August 7, 140 fighter-bombers, 367 light bombers and 187 medium bombers came down heavily on Adrano.

The advance of the ground troops towards Randazzo was accompanied by intense air attacks. The town itself quickly became one of the most heavily bombed targets in Sicily. The peak of the bomber effort was reached on August 7, when 104 Mitchell and 142 Boston Americans, along with Boston and Baltimore of the RAF and SAAF, destroyed most of the town. Between August 1 and 13, a total of 425 medium bombers, 248 light bombers and 72 fighter bombers had attacked the city.

On the island, the German army under the orders of General Hube successfully implemented the retreat through three defensive lines, taking advantage of the narrowing of the Sicilian territory as it approached Messina. The Germans sabotaged all the vehicles before abandoning them, burning everything they could spare. On the two sides of the Strait, the Sicilian and the Calabrian, the most impressive concentration of anti-aircraft emplacements was set up, the fearsome 88 mm Flak cannons. For the defense of the Strait of Messina, Oberst Ernst-Günther Baade put in place as many as five hundred gun ports located on both sides.

On August 10, he completed his work, with the placement of all artillery budgeted and with the preparation of ten well camouflaged and prepared landings, able to accommodate the fleet of barges and motor boats, which would lead men and materials in Calabria.

Randazzo fell the 11 August; to the Italian-German troops did not remain that to cross quickly the Strait of Messina to retire in the continent.

To coordinate the naval operations for the evacuation from the island it was chosen the Captain of Vessel Gustav Freiherr von Liebenstein, already decorated with cross of knight. At his orders he had three transport flotillas of the Kriegsmarine, similar units of the army, and some armed pontoons of the Luftwaffe, as well as Italian ships of various sizes[11].

This heterogeneous fleet managed by five battalions of engineers was able to transport 8,000 men and 2,000 tons of materials and equipment every night.

At dawn on 17 August, the evacuation of the island was a complete German success. In the course of the 5 days only few naval means and some pontoon Siebel had been lost. This was the end of what Allied military historians called the *Italian-German Dunkirk* and which, it should be remembered, took place for the Italian and German armies at the same time but in parallel, as the Axis forces each jealously committed their own means to evacuate the island.

On the home front, the most intense and spectacular air battle of the month took place on Monday, August 16, during an attack on the Foggia airport complex by B-24 Liberators of the 9th Air Force. Between 75 and 100 Italian-German fighters engaged in a long fight with the Liberators and the air escort; eight American four-engine aircraft, seven of which belonged to the 44th Bombardment Group and one to the 376th Bombardment Group, were lost in the battle, but claimed the destruction of forty-five enemy fighters. These aerial actions carried out in the final phase of Operation Husky brought the actual sorties to 4,846 and the bombs dropped to 8,009 tons[12].

The fall of Sicily was sealed by the entrance of the 3rd Infantry Division of the Seventh U.S. Army of General Patton, which at 10:00 a.m. on August 17 triumphantly entered Messina, followed by the British troops of General Montgomery. The conquest of Sicily in thirty-eight days was in many ways a model campaign. In it, land, air and sea forces had been combined.

---

11 The main craft was the Siebel pontoon or Siebelfähre, a type of vessel designed in 1940 by the aeronautical engineer Siebel, often armed with 20 mm Flak anti-aircraft guns for self-defense, some were converted to floating anti-aircraft batteries with 88 mm Flak guns. It consisted of two heavy-duty deck elements with propulsion provided by self-propelled engines, with a displacement of 130 tons, a fully loaded speed of 6-7 knots, and a carrying capacity of 50 tons and 150-200 men.
12 For these data the missions operated by all Allied air units against Italian, Sardinian and Sicilian airports between July 4 and August 17 were taken into consideration.

FROM THE BOMBING OF ROME TO THE BRENNER PASS

At 2:30 a.m. in the morning of July 25, after ten hours of discussion, the majority of the hierarchs of the Great Council of Fascism had voted no confidence in the Duce, Benito Mussolini. At 17.30 of the same day Mussolini was arrested by the Carabinieri, thus decreeing the end of the fascist regime.

The Badoglio government had already asked the United States, through the Vatican, to know the essential conditions to obtain the status of *open city* for Rome; Eisenhower had to wait for further instructions before authorizing a second bombing. Of course, the hypothesis of granting Rome the status of *open city* had aroused the violent opposition of Churchill, who had pointed out to Roosevelt its political inappropriateness since it would have been taken as proof that the Allies were *abandoning the principle of unconditional surrender*[13].

On Sunday, August 1, Operation Tidal Wave got underway; 177 Consolidated B-24 Liberators belonging to five different groups of the 8th and 9th Air Force of the USAAF flew a mission to destroy the oil refineries of Ploieşti in Romania, which were essential for the supply of fuel to the German armed forces. The four-engine aircraft departed from bases around Benghazi, Libya reached Romania to carry out a low-altitude attack on the refineries. Although the damage to the production plants was extensive, the price paid by the American formations was very high, in a disastrous operation that led to the loss of 41 bombers and a total of 532 formation crews.

At 11.00 a.m. on Friday 13 August Rome was hit for the second time by American planes arriving in geometric formations. This time only the aircrafts of the 12th Air Force USAAF, which took off from the airports of Tunisia and Algeria[14], took part in the mission and were accompanied by escort fighters coming from Pantelleria airport and from the Sicilian bases. In addition to the 106 B-17 Flying Fortresses escorted by 45 P-38 Lightnings, there were 102 B-26 Marauders and 66 B-25 Mitchells escorted by 90 P-38 Lightning fighters. A total of 409 aircraft flew over the capital at various altitudes, and in less than an hour unloaded 500 tons of explosives, which was half the amount of bombs that had been dropped during the first attack on July 19. On the B-17 *Dirty Gertie* of the 32nd Bombardment Squadron, 301st Bombardment Group USAAF, General Doolittle had embarked himself.

The second bombing of Rome was part of the offensive unleashed by the US Air Force in the Mediterranean since the beginning of August to prepare the ground for the path towards its conquest. The plan included large-scale bombings against ports, stations, airports, railway lines and communication routes. From a political point of view, it was clear that, by now, Eisenhower, in agreement with his government and the British, was trying to accelerate Badoglio's decision to sign an armistice and bring Italy out of the conflict.

The primary objectives of the Flying Fortresses were to "overhaul" the Littorio and Ciampino airports, the San Lorenzo freight terminal and the Tuscolana station, and to wipe out the marshalling yards at Prenestina and Casilina stations.

---

13 Roosevelt Churchill, *Carteggio segreto di guerra*, A. Mondadori Editore, Milano 1977, p. 407.
14 The B-24 Liberators of the 9th Air Force did not carry out any missions because they were rather debilitated after the losses suffered during the famous and costly August 1 raid on the oil installations at Ploieşti.

On the morning of August 14, less than 24 hours after the bombing, the Badoglio government declared Rome an *open city*. It was the Foreign Minister Raffaele Guariglia to communicate it to the governments of London and Washington, and to the neutral countries. While Sicily was falling, the 8th Air Force USAAF in Great Britain set up a large-scale attack on one of the most ambitious targets ever carried out in Europe. The intent was to cripple the German aircraft industry with what would go down in history as the first raid on Schweinfurt-Regensburg in Germany. The first formation of 127 Boeing B-17 Flying Fortress heavy bombers, with no fighter escort, managed to drop 299 tons of bombs on the target before losing 24 B-17s to German fighters. A second wave of 183 American B-17 bombers arrived on the same target a few hours later; they paid an even higher price with 36 bombers shot down and 121 damaged.

At the same time in Italy over a hundred NASAF bombers attacked Battipaglia and Castrovillari, heavily escorted by P-38 Lightnings. On August 19 Luftwaffe planes that had withdrawn to "safer" air bases in the Foggia area had to face the arrival of about 150 B-17 and 70 B-24 in separate formations, while over 100 medium bombers hit Salerno and Sapri.

On August 31 the 9th Air Force sent B-24s to bomb the railway station of Pescara; on the same day about 150 B-17s bombed the railway station of Pisa. In the meantime A-20 and B-25 medium and light bombers attacked at low and medium altitudes roads and railway lines near Catanzaro, and in the afternoon the city of Cosenza; fighter-bombers went on a mission over the seaplane base and the railway line near Sapri.

On the 2nd of September the communications with the Brenner pass and Trento were temporarily blocked by the bombs of the American bombers; if the operation had been more energetic, continuous, and above all carried out in due time, it could perhaps have delayed the arrival in Italy of the powerful German occupation force, which first the weak Italian government and then the Allied commands had to deal with. In the afternoon of the same day, 76 B-17 Flying Fortresses attacked Bologna, unloading 187 tons of bombs, reducing the large railway station to ashes and damaging the historical center of the city.

On the other side of the strait, the month began trying to weaken the Italian-German rearguards in Calabria, with the bombing also by medium and light bombers of the NATAF of road and rail bridges and also some Radar stations.

At 04.30 a.m. of September 3, 1943 (a day also marked by the signing of the Italian armistice) a heavy bombardment began on the coast between Reggio Calabria and Villa San Giovanni; at 05.40 a.m. two divisions of the British Eighth Army landed on the Calabrian coast, the British Fifth Division and the Canadian First Division: thus began Operation Baytown. The German resistance was almost non-existent because the troops had retreated inland between the peaks of the Calabrian Apennines, as they had decided to organize the defenses further north. At 07.30 a.m. the other boats sailed from Santa Teresa di Riva, thus concluding the embarkation.

Operation Baytown had been decided since August 14, 1943, when the Allies had found that the port of Messina was unserviceable because of German sabotage, and that consequently it would have been difficult for the bulk of the forces to reach the city of the Strait because of the fact that in the highway between Catania and Messina the retreating Germans had blown up with dynamite some bridges.

About Operation Baytown, wrote "L'Avvenire d'Italia": "The enemy renews the tactical plan tested in Sicily: systematic air attack on all rail lines, military ganglia, production centers, through raids that in recent weeks day and night have traveled, breathless, our charming provinces of the south.

On September 3, Marshal Badoglio informed for the first time officially the Chiefs of Staff of the Army, Navy and Air Force that his government was negotiating an armistice with the Allies, which would become effective no earlier than September 12[15].

However, negotiations with the Allies should not have been a mystery to the Italian generals, since on the morning of September 2 Castellano had returned from Sicily aboard an airplane piloted by Major Giovanni Vassallo of the General Staff of the Air Force, who had also been part of the Italian delegation, not to mention the previous contacts with the Allies and other flights to Sicily that had been recorded since the end of August.

On the afternoon of September 3, in a military tent among the olive trees of Cassibile, in the Syracuse area, the flashes of the photographic lenses and the cold eye of the camera immortalized, in a brief ceremony, with the cordiality that the circumstances demanded, the signing of an armistice that put an end to the war between Italy and the Anglo-Americans. The signatures, affixed at 17.15, were of the Brigadier General, attached to the Italian Supreme Command, Giuseppe Castellano, representing the Italian Marshal Pietro Badoglio, Head of Government, and of the General of the American Army and Chief of Staff, Walter Bedell-Smith, representing the Commander in Chief of the Allied forces Dwight Eisenhower.

A first draft of the conditions to be imposed on Italy had been sent from London to Washington on July 29, and the 17 articles had been reduced under pressure from the Americans. The Allies had then elaborated in Quebec, between 14 and 24 August, the explanatory and interpretative text in 44 articles, which will become the so-called *long armistice*[16].

The armistice was then made public at 19.45 on 8 September by the microphones of EIAR, which interrupted broadcasting to transmit the announcement, previously recorded, of General Badoglio announcing the surrender to the nation.

After the signing of the armistice, General Mark Wayne Clark, to whom went the command of the American Fifth Army, was informed by Eisenhower of the surrender of Italy, and the end of the Italian-German alliance.

The American command planned to launch near Rome the 82nd Parachute Division, code-named Operation Giant II. This operation, however, was strongly conditioned by the co-operation of the Italian forces, who would have had the task of occupying the airports of Guidonia, Littoria, Cerveteri and Furbara, and make them available to the paratroopers. Unfortunately for Badoglio, things became more complicated due to the strong presence of the former German ally in Rome.

A message from Badoglio followed, saying: "Due to the changes in the situation, which has clearly worsened, and due to the presence of German forces in the area of Rome, it is no longer possible to announce the armistice because the capital would be occupied and power would be assumed by force by the Germans. The operation is no longer possible because I do not have the necessary forces to maintain the airports".

---

15 Ruggero Zangrandi, *1943: l'8 settembre*, Feltrinelli editore, Milano, 1967, p. 82.
16 Marco Patricelli, *op. cit.*, p. 272.

Meanwhile, the preparations for the conquest of Salerno, codenamed Operation Avalanche, discussed and finalized on August 23 in Algiers, were now in their final stages. The British Eighth Army would act as a diversion, while the main effort would be made by the American Fifth Army at Salerno. The landing force would consist of General Ernest Dawley's U.S. VI Corps. These forces were to capture Naples and join Montgomery's British Eighth Army, rising from Calabria.

In all, the Anglo-American forces could count on about 30,000 British soldiers and 25,000 Americans to attack the German positions, defended by about 20,000 men, already deployed in the area of Salerno, while another 100,000 were the enemies that the Allies believed could converge in the area of the landings in a short time.

Above all, the 16th Panzer-Division, led by German General Heinrich von Vietinghoff, which had four units, all at a short distance from the bridgehead, had to be countered: after the experience in Sicily, in fact, von Vietinghoff decided not to fight on the beaches, but to strengthen his forces and attack by exploiting the highest positions. Thus, it was decided that the XIV Panzerkorps would be deployed to the north against the British forces of the X Corps, while the LXXVI Panzerkorps would engage the Americans south of the Sele River. The Hermann Göring Armored Division, returning from Sicily and reinforced by elements of the 1st Fallschirmjäger Division, along with the 15th Panzergrenadier Division, deployed north on the Gulf of Gaeta but severely short of armor, were ordered to move toward the bridgehead as early as the evening of September 9.

On September 5, about 130 B-17 Flying Fortresses attacked the airfields of Civitavecchia and Viterbo; more than 200 B-25 Mitchells and B-26 Marauders were directed against the airfields around Grazzanise, in Campania. In the early hours of September 9 Fifth Army troops set foot on the beaches of Salerno, officially starting Operation Avalanche, while in the afternoon 41 B-24s bombed the runways of Foggia, and B-17s attacked road bridges near Cancello Arnone and Capua; more than 240 sorties were made by B-25s and B-26s against railroad bridges in Potenza and the airstrip at Scanzano. On the 10th, Flying Fortresses, Mitchells and Marauders went to support ground operations in the Salerno area; meanwhile B-24 Liberators did not let go of their grip on the Foggia airport complex. At 07.40 a.m. of the same day, a formation of 12 A-36A Invader fighters of the 27th Fighter-Bomber Group in armed reconnaissance spotted more than 500 enemy armored vehicles and craft near Lagonegro, marching north about 70 miles from Salerno. A few moments after the identification the formation carried out a dive attack, bombing and strafing the long column; the attackers estimated that they destroyed about 177 German vehicles and damaged another 246.

On 11 September, 16 German Dornier Do 217K2 bombers of III./KG 100 attacked the cruisers USS *Philadelphia* and *Savannah* and their escort while supporting Allied forces at Salerno. The Savannah was hit by a German FX 1400 radio-controlled bomb, known to the Allies as Fritz-X.

With the conquest of the first airfields on the Italian peninsula, the American Spitfires of the 31st Fighter Group were able to take position at Montecorvino airfield on 20 September, followed by the fighter-bombers of the 27th and 86th Fighter-Bomber Group at Sele airfield on 26 September.

After ten days of bitter fighting, the Allies, who had suffered much higher losses than the Germans, were able to emerge from the quagmire and reorganize in view of the advance toward Naples, which would be conquered only on October 1, 1943. The Germans, at the same time, preferred to retreat in an orderly manner toward the north in direction of the fortified line, denominated Volturno Line, castled in the impervious Apennine territory to north of the Campania's chief town, where they prepared themselves to face the Allies in advance.

During the first week of October, the Tactical Bomber Force made about 2,600 sorties in support of the Fifth and Eighth Armies. In the first two days, 160 American P-40s had paved the way for the Eighth Army's landing at Termoli on the Adriatic, bombing and strafing troops and vehicles on roads northwest of the city. On October 3, the day of the capture of Benevento, and the following day, in spite of the bad weather, the fighter-bombers, together with the B-25s, inflicted heavy damages to the German movements. On the 13th of October, in Brindisi, the Badoglio government formally declared war on Germany; this decision would have caused the clear division of what remained of the Regia Aeronautica into two parts: the Aeronautica Cobelligerante, allied to the Anglo-American forces, and the Aeronautica Nazionale Repubblicana, loyal to the German ally.

On October 19, and for the next five days, the bridges and railroad system of central Italy came under attack. Medium and heavy bombers made more than 650 sorties, dropping about 1,350 tons of bombs. The damage to rail traffic north of the Rome area was extensive and required extensive repairs. The Germans were forced to rely on road and sea supplies. On the 21st, the B-17s bombed a railway viaduct at Terni; the B-24s targeted a railway bridge near Orvieto and the B-25s and B-26s the same type of target, but between Acquapendente and Montalto di Castro; not even the railway line at Orbetello was spared. The Lightning were left with the task of hitting a Radar station near Pellegrino. The NATAF diverted A-20 and B-25s to enemy troop concentrations near Cassino and the surrounding areas.

On Oct. 24, the Air Force sent medium bombers over Tirana airfield in Albania and heavy bombers over Austria. Here, 89 B-17s and 25 B-24s, escorted by 36 P-38s, bombed the German Messerschmitt Bf 109 fighter factory at Wiener-Neustadt. With the target completely covered by clouds, only the B-24s of the 98th Bombardment Group were able to hit the primary target. The B-17s of the 301st Bombardment Group attacked the railroad yard north of Wiener-Neustadt[17].

On 29 October in Washington, General Marshall met with General Eisenhower and suggested that an intensification of medium and light bomber and fighter-bomber operations was vital to the advance of the Fifth and Eighth Armies, leaving the heavy bombers free to attack the railroad lines and bridges of the Po Valley and targets further away from the front.

---

17 Hammel Eric, *Air War Europe. American's air war against Germany in Europe and North Africa. Chronology 1942-1945*, Pacifica Press, USA, 1994, p. 199.

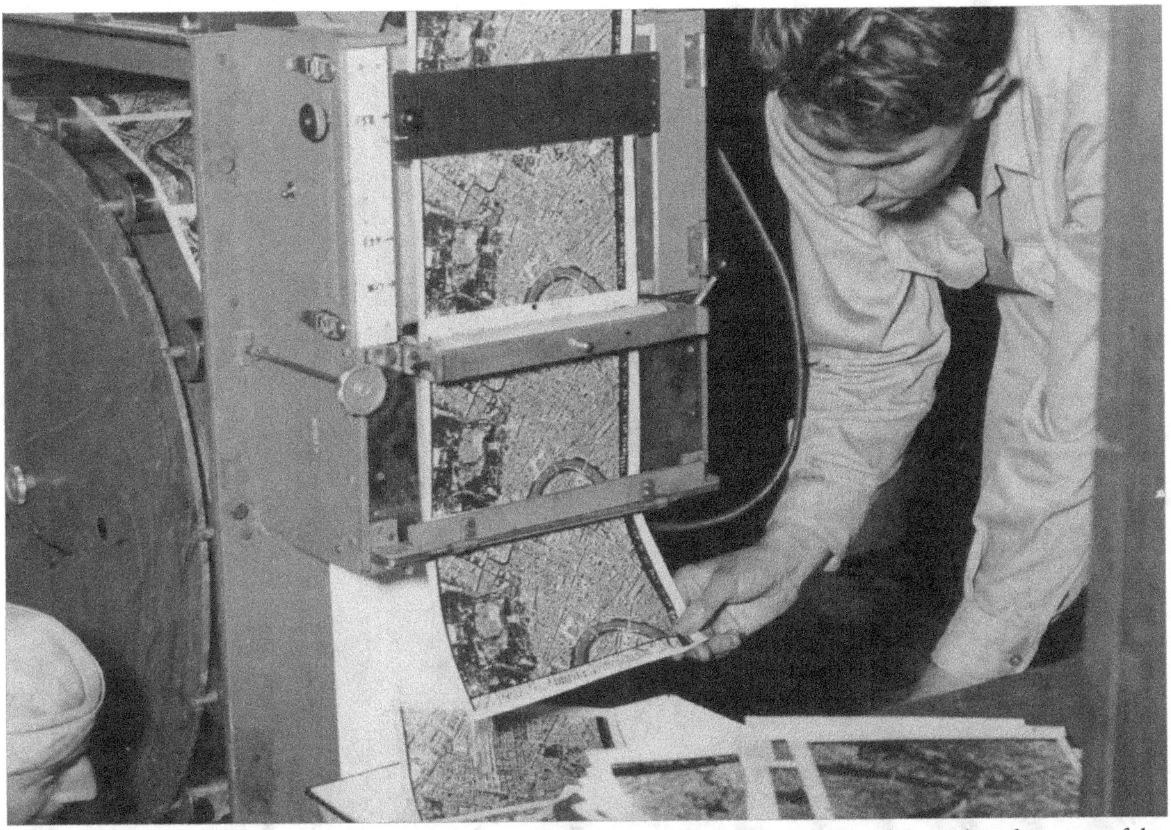

▲ Duplicate photos of Rome taken by Allied aerial reconnaissance. You can see Villa Borghese and, in the center of the picture, Via del Corso diagonally.

▼ The formation of Boeing B-17 Flying Fortresses of the 301st BG in flight, heading to attack Viterbo airport on July 29, 1943.

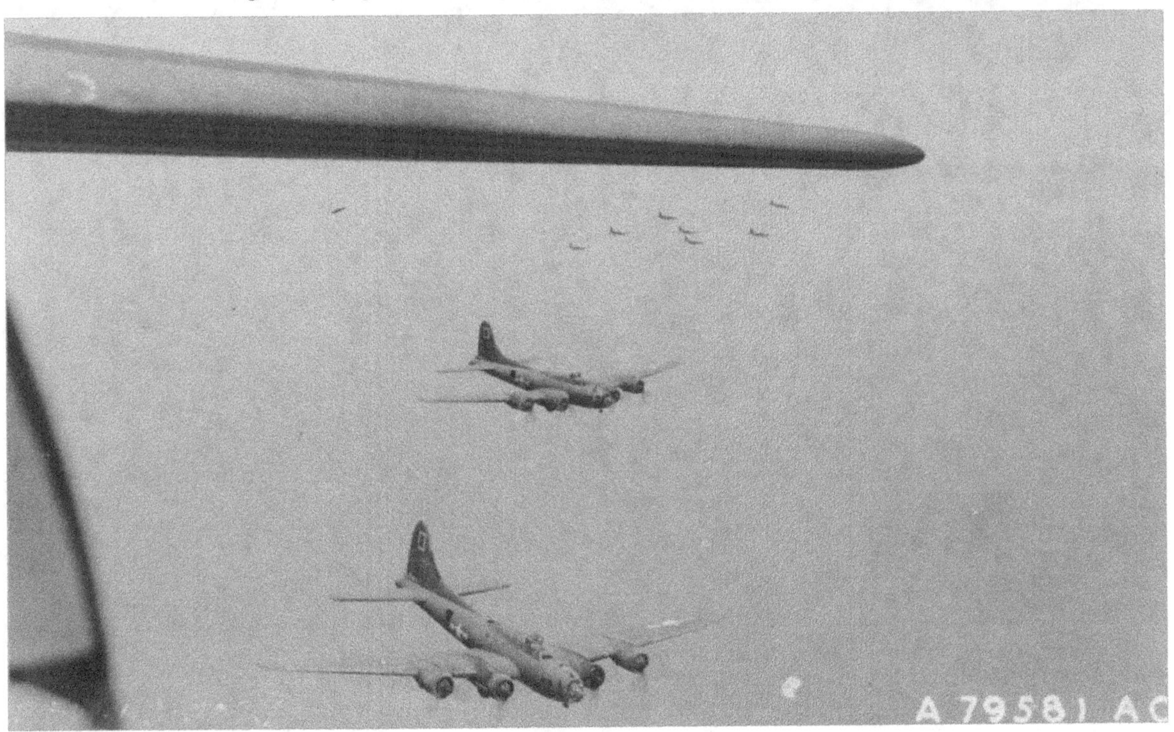

▲ The Foggia train station and part of the city bombed on July 22, 1943 by B-17s of the 97th BG. On that occasion the B-17F s/n 42-30119 "Hunter's Answer" piloted by 2nd Lieutenant Frank H. Hunter of the 346th BS was hit and shot down by anti-aircraft fire.

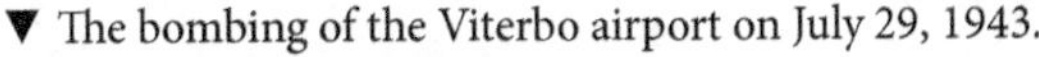

▲ The tragic moment when the B-17F s/n 42-30119 "Hunter's Answer" is hit on one of the engines by anti-aircraft fire.

▼ The bombing of the Viterbo airport on July 29, 1943.

▲ Bombing of Benevento railway station by 36 B-25 Mitchell of the 321st BG escorted by 31 P-38 of the 82nd FG, followed by 36 B-25 of the 310th BG on August 27, 1943.

▼ The North American B-25C Mitchell s/n 41-12480 "Desert Warrior" belonging to the 81st BS, 12th BG. In the foreground is Captain Ralph M. Lower and his crew.

▲ The crew of the B-17F s/n 42-5456 "Adele's Angel," piloted by Captain E. M. Slack Jr. and belonging to the 419th BS, 301st BG. The entire crew poses behind a device to celebrate their 100th mission. Here returning from the bombing of Livorno.

▼ Bomb Fall Plot of the bombing raid on Naples on 1 August 1943. The raid was carried out by B-17 Flying Fortresses of the 99th BG.

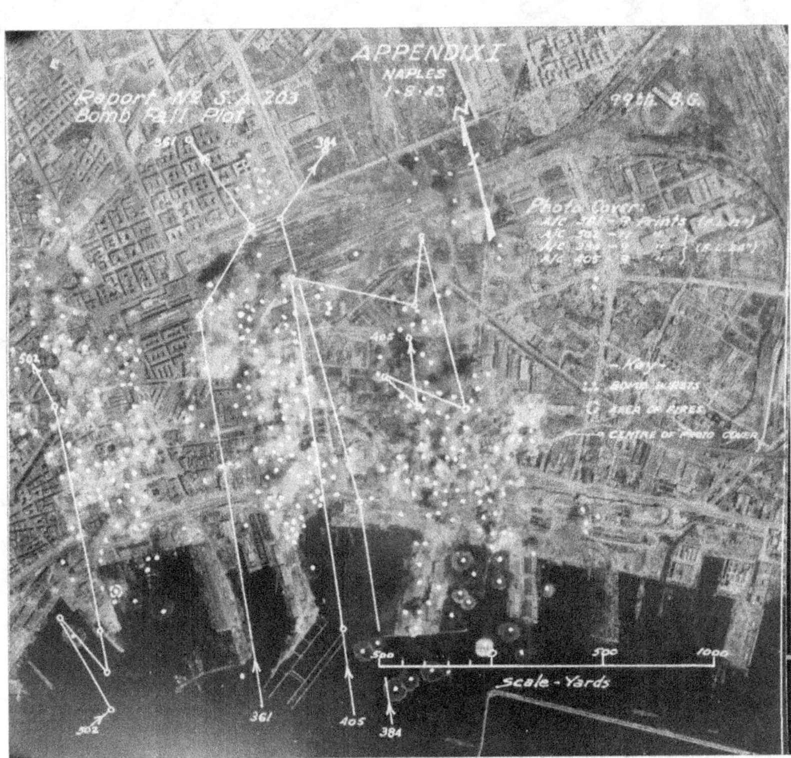

▲ Photo of Pisa taken on September 2, 1943 by a Mosquito PR from 60 Squadron SAAF. Photo shows marked ordnance impact points and data from the attached Interpretation Report.

▲ Photo taken over Rome on June 19, 1943 by an F-5A reconnaissance aircraft of the 3rd Photographic Reconnaissance Group USAAF.

▼ A formation of B-26 Marauders flies over Rome. In the foreground is the B-26B s/n 41-18275 "Little Salvo" belonging to the 320th BG.

▲ The bombing of the railway station of San Lorenzo in Rome in the summer of 1943.

▲ Different view of the B-26 Marauder over the Capital.

▼ From left, Colonel Elliot Roosevelt leading the NAPRW, and General Harold Alexander, pointing to some targets on the map of Italy with his right hand.

▲ Colonel Keith K. Compton CO of the 376th BG (left bent over) and Major N. V. Arnold in a briefing before a mission over Austria.

▼ Colonel Keith K. Compton (center), and Brigadier General Uzal G. Ent (right) commander of IX Bomber Command, pictured in front of B-24D s/n 42-40664 "Teggie Ann", a leading aircraft in the attack on the refineries at Ploiesti, Romania. This bomber would be shot down during the raid on Foggia on 16 August 1943.

▲ The air raid on Capua on September 9, 1943. On that occasion a railway bridge and two road bridges were hit by B-17s of the 347th BS, 99th BG.

▲ On September 17, 1943 the Ciampino airport suffered a heavy attack by B-17 and B-26 of the NASAF.

▲ In the foreground a large bomb with its governor at the moment of the launch on the airport of Udine. The first American bombing raid on Udine was carried out on 25 December 1943 by B-24s of the 9th Air Force.

▲ Image of the bombing of the Bologna train station on September 2, 1943 by B-17 Flying Fortress of the 97th BG.

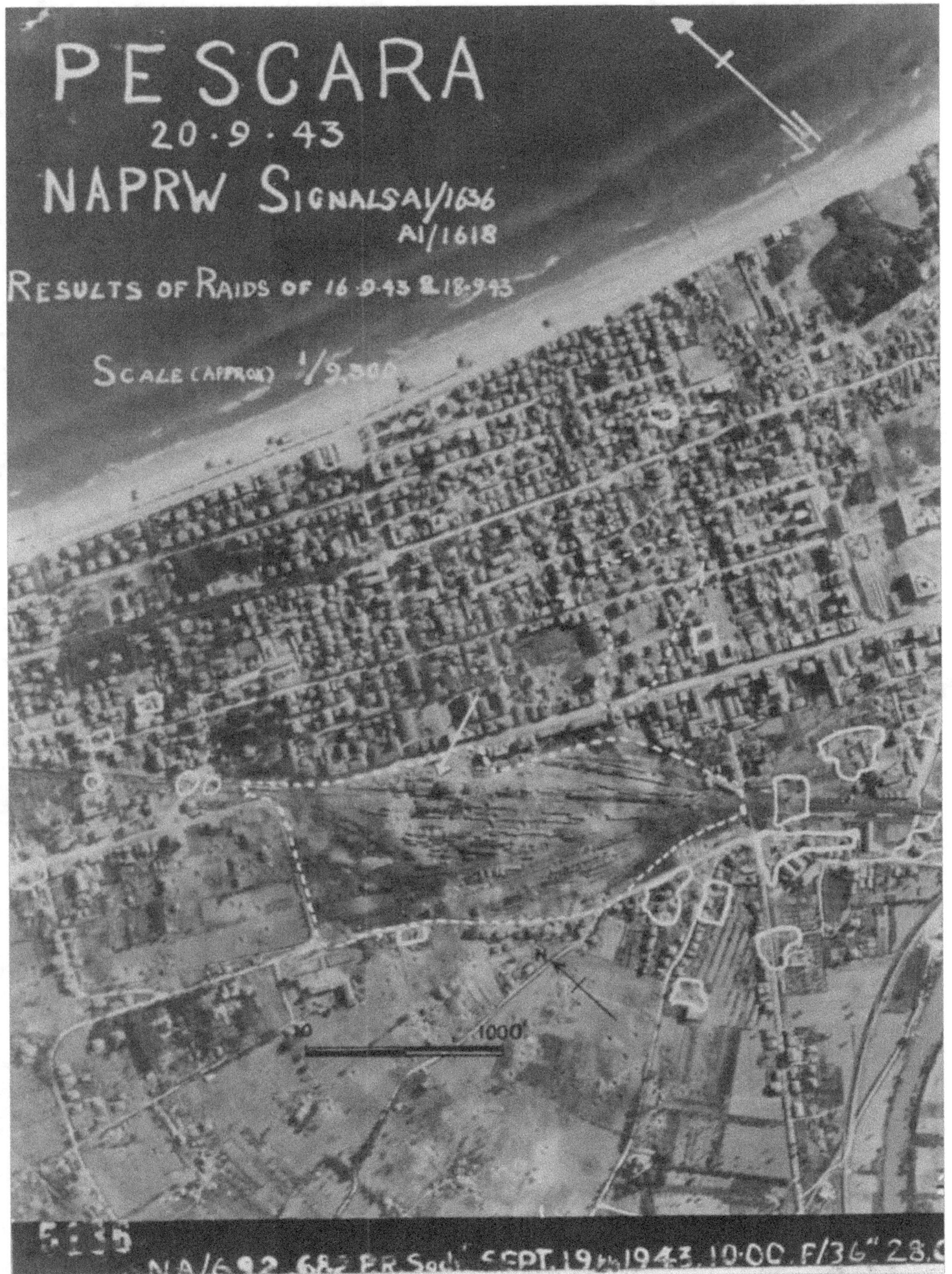

▲ Photogram taken on 19 September 1943 over Pescara by a Spitfire PR of 682 Squadron RAF, which was assigned the task of checking the damage of the American bombing raids on the railway station on 16 and 18 September 1943.

▲ Bolzano train station bombed on November 10, 1943 by B-17 Flying Fortresses of the 15th Air Force.

THE 15TH USAAF AIR FORCE IN ITALY

At the end of 1943, Italy's ascent was bogged down by the preliminary German defense fronts of the Gustav Line, which cut the peninsula at its narrowest point, between the Garigliano and Sangro rivers, from Gaeta to Ortona passing through the Liri valley and Cassino.

On the western side, Clark's Fifth Army operated, on the eastern side Montgomery's Eighth Army: both of them had to face the terrible Apennine winter, of which they had no knowledge, and Kasselring on the opposite front, who continuously moved the German units as if they were mere pawns.

In the meantime, in Moscow the Allied Foreign Ministers met in what will go down in history as the third Moscow conference, in which they discussed which collaborations and measures should be undertaken to shorten and end the war with Germany and the Axis powers.

In Italy, the attention of the USAAF air force shifted against a new set of targets further to the northwest, close to the French border.

On October 29 and 30, American bombers reached the coast of Liguria. Genoa, already hit on the 29th by the Flying Fortresses, was hit the following day by twenty B-24 Liberators, which hit the railway station, the Ansaldo steelworks and other industrial plants; the Sampierdarena district, however, suffered the most. On the 30th, 133 Flying Fortresses dropped bombs on Imperia, Porto Maurizio, Savona and Varazze; while NATAF B-25s attacked Frosinone, and some fighter units, such as the P-40s of the 324th Fighter Group, moved from Tunisia to Cercola airport, in Campania, to join other elements of the 12th ASC.

On 1 November, the Luftwaffe attacked Naples, leaving behind 144 dead. The bombing caused serious damage to the Spanish quarters, where there were collapses in vico Tofa and in via Gesù e Maria, considerable damage and victims also among Allied soldiers in vico Canale, gradini San Matteo and vico Lungo Montecalvario[18].

From November 1 was formally established the 15th Air Force, based in Tunis[19]. The heavy bombing units were transferred to it, with the B-17 and B-24 of the 9th and 12th Air Force, which formed the 5th Bombardment Wing. This air force was based mainly in Apulia and in the Foggia airfields; the B-26s and P-38s of the 42nd Bombardment Wing went to Sardinia, and the 47th Bombardment Wing, with B-25s and P-38s, to Manduria in the heel of Italy. Strengthened by the complete dominance of the air over southern Italy, an advanced group of the new area force settled in Bari, and on November 22 transfer orders were issued for all remaining operational sites with the order to reach Italy as early as November 30. The movement was completed on December 3, except for some aliquots that completed the transfer at the end of December.

---

18 Gribaudi Gabriella, *Guerra totale. Tra bombe alleate e violenze naziste. Napoli e il fronte meridionale 1940-1944*, Bollati Boringhieri, 2005, p. 160.

19 It was an imposing air force which, at the peak of its operations, had 21 heavy bomber groups (6 of B-17 and 15 of B-24) and seven fighter groups (3 of P-38, 3 of P-51 and one of P-47) in function and escort to the bombing groups, and numerous other minor units.

On December 1ˢᵗ the Tunis base was officially closed and the Bari base was opened, where the 15ᵗʰ Air Force remained until the end of the Italian Campaign[20].

In the last two weeks of November the weather conditions worsened, so as to prevent most of the missions. On the 19ᵗʰ some missions were operated by A-36A and P-40 in the area of Cassino and Pontecorvo, with the attack of some bridges and trains near Rieti. On the 26ᵗʰ, 27ᵗʰ and 28ᵗʰ the conditions returned partially favorable, which favored the attack of B-17 and B-24 heavy bombers on the areas of Rimini, Grizzano and Vergato; on the 29ᵗʰ the airports in the area of Rome and Grosseto were bombed. Medium and light bombers targeted enemy positions near the mountain towns around Mignano, below Cassino, and south of Cerveteri and Valmontone.

Incursions were registered against the docks of Civitavecchia and the port of Anzio. The month ended with the bombing of Fiume by B-24s of the 15ᵗʰ Air Force.

On December 2 the Luftwaffe attacked undisturbed the port of Bari. On the evening of December 2, 1943, 105 Junkers Ju 88 bombers, belonging to the German Luftflotte 2, bombed Allied transport ships loaded with ammunition anchored at anchor in the port; the attack caused great losses for the Allies, who had not suffered a surprise air raid of such effectiveness and intensity on one of their ports since the Japanese attack of Pearl Harbor.

The bombs hit the SS *John L. Motley* and the SS *John Harvey*, which exploded inside the port area full of ships; the subsequent explosions, and the resulting fires, destroyed seventeen ships for a total of 62,000 tons. Due to the very serious damage it took three weeks to return to normal.

During the last half of December, the strategic bombers intensified their offensive against the railway lines; on 16 December the B-24s attacked a railway tunnel between Dogna and Chiusaforte, and the B-17s bombed the station and the railway intersections at Padua. Despite the bad weather, which cancelled many missions, the heavy bombers managed to complete 812 sorties, and the B-26s 737.

The line of the main targets was now established in the area of the Brenner and Tarvisio on which the four-engine aircraft operated; the targets on the west and east coast lines were instead entrusted to the twin-engine aircraft. On the Brenner line in the yards of Innsbruck and Bolzano, and on the viaduct over the Avisio river between Trento and Bolzano, a total of 450 tons of bombs were dropped.

The attacks did not stop even on Christmas Day, when the B-24s of the 376ᵗʰ Bombardment Group bombed the Udine train station and the Vicenza airport, sensationally missing the latter, and hitting homes in the suburbs caused a total of 31 casualties. The B-17s further attacked the Udine train station and the Bolzano train station. B-26 Marauders of the 15ᵗʰ Air Force bombed several railway stations between Pisa and Porta Nuova.

---

20 This new reorganization had brought into the 15ᵗʰ Air Force, by the end of December, from an initial staff of 3,624 officers and 16,875 enlisted men a combined total of 4,873 officers and 32,867 enlisted men. Craven Wesley Frank and Cate James Lea, op. cit., p. 571.

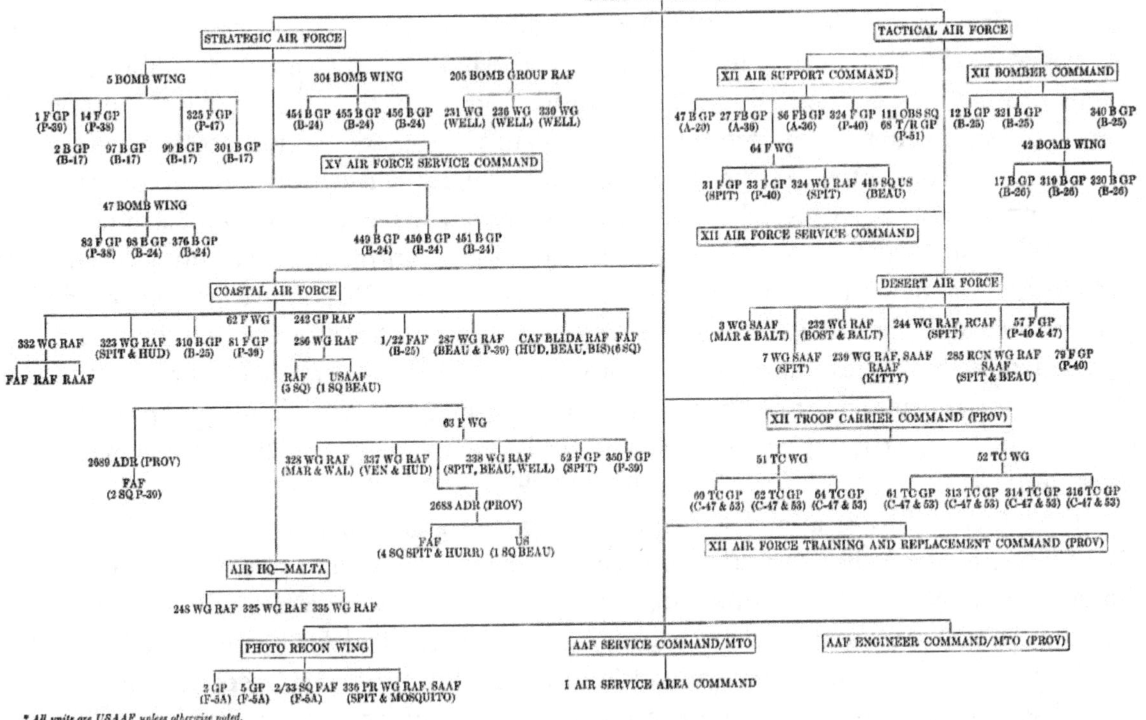

* All units are USAAF unless otherwise noted.

▲ Some American aircraft at the Palermo Boccadifalco airport. A B-17, a C-47 and some P-38 Lightning can be seen. The circle on the drift identifies the B-17 as belonging to the 2nd BG.

THE LANDING AT ANZIO

The beginning of the new year marked a radical change in the Allied leadership of the entire Mediterranean theater. The American Air Force, that had consolidated its positions in Italy, was now called to manage more frequently the missions on the other side of the border, on Austria, France and Germany; to the east, the sorties on the Yugoslavian front were also intensified. To the generals, that had egregiously carried out important military campaigns, it was ordered to return to England; the General Dwight Eisenhower assumed the position of supreme Allied commander for the imminent invasion of Normandy, and the Air Marshal Sir Arthur Tedder was named his vice. Eisenhower was succeeded by General Sir Henry Maitland-Wilson, nicknamed "Jumbo"; born in London, he had a long experience in the Middle East. General Sir Bernard Montgomery would have the task of commanding the army during the initial phases of the Normandy landings, as well as Air Vice Marshal Sir Arthur Coningham, who took command of the 2nd Tactical Air Force. The command of the Mediterranean Allied Air Forces (MAAF), meanwhile, passed to the American General Ira Clarence Eaker, coming from the 8th Air Force USAAF in England. Major General James H. Doolittle, however, passed the command of the 15th Air Force to Major General Nathan F. Twining. The Eighth Army was taken over by General Sir Oliver Leese, and at the same time the command of the Allied Tactical Air Force in the Mediterranean was assigned to American General John Kenneth Cannon. The reorganization of the USAAF elements in the Mediterranean was now practically complete. By January, the 12th Air Force had become a purely tactical arm and secondary to the 15th Air Force, of which it had incorporated the former medium bomber groups[21].

When General Eaker arrived in the Mediterranean, on January 14, 1944, there was only one week left before Operation Shingle, the planned landing at Anzio, which would involve a force of American and British troops totaling about 110,000.

The ground troops of the US VI Corps under Major General John Lucas, composed of the First British Infantry Division under the command of General Penney and the Third Infantry Division under Major General Lucian Truscott, were to secure the bridgehead and then advance towards the Colli Laziali, about seven miles inland; a promontory would give them command over the Anzio plain and roads 6 and 7, the two main communication arteries for the German troops, who would probably move from Rome towards the battle zone.

Shortly before the landing, the Fifth Army put in action a strong attack with the purpose of breaking the Gustav Line, marching then towards the Liri Valley to rejoin as in a vice with the forces on the Latium coast. The Eighth Army would have had the task of operating along the front of eastern Italy to prevent the transfer of German troops to the other sectors of operations. Alerted to the possible Anglo-American operations, Field Marshal Kesselring placed the 92. Infanterie-Division, and to the south the 4. Fallschirmjäger-Division, while the 29. and 90. Panzergrenadier were placed in mobile reserve to counter possible landings. Only later did Kesselring move his pawns at night to avoid Anglo-American air

---

21 The 15th Air Force, starting from the complex of airfields located in Puglia, managed to reach all the oil refineries in southern Europe, attacking enemy aircraft factories within its range, and destroying 6,282 enemy aircraft in the air and on the ground.

attacks during the day. The experienced Panzer-Division Hermann Göring positioned itself in front of the American regiments, the 3. Panzergrenadier-Division was responsible for the section in front of Campoleone, defended by the British, and the 65. Infanterie-Division was finally assigned to the realization of a defensive line beyond the Moletta river. From the front of Cassino the 29. and the 90. Panzergrenadier-Division.

The responsibility for the air support would have fallen largely on the Tactical Air Force, which, by bombing the airports, would have prevented the Luftwaffe from interfering in the amphibious operations, also maintaining constant pressure on the lines of communication between Rome and northern Italy. The six U.S. groups of the XII Bomber Command composed of B-25s and B-26s, would have interdicted the connections between Rome and the Pisa-Florence line, while the fighters and fighter-bombers of the XII ASC and Desert Air Force engaged in close support the ground troops.

On January 2, forty-three B-25s of the 57th Bombardment and seventy-three B-26s of the 42nd Bombardment Wing attacked the railroad east of Nice; the results were satisfactory, especially at Taggia, where a railroad bridge was destroyed, and at Ventimiglia, where the two spans of the bridge were totally blown up, with Republic P-47 Thunderbolts of the 325th Fighter Group in free fighter flight over Rome. The following day, fifty B-17s of the 97th and 301st Bombardment Group of the 15th Air Force severely damaged the Lingotto railroad yard in Turin, Italy, while another fifty-three Flying Fortresses of the 2nd and 99th Bombardment Group dealt a heavy blow to the industrial plants at Villar Perosa in the Turin area.

In the first two days of the month, about fifty A-36As of the XII Air Support Command had hit the docks of Civitavecchia, for some time a favorite destination because it was the closest port to Rome and the battle front.

On 8 January, one hundred and nine Flying Fortresses came upon the aircraft and fighter aircraft assembly and construction plants in Reggio Emilia, severely damaging them, including the nearby railroad lines.

On the 19th and 20th heavy bombers, mainly B-17s, carried out intense bombing raids on airports in the Rome area, dropping 700 tons of bombs in 191 sorties against Ciampino North and South, 103 against Centocelle and 56 against Guidonia.

On January 22, 1944, the US VI Army Corps landed on the beaches of Anzio. The German forces, under the command of Field Marshal Albert Kesselring, in spite of a timid initial surprise, managed to reorganize quickly and to block the Allied advance, launching a series of counterattacks that put the Anglo-Americans in serious difficulty and cost them heavy losses. The long and wearisome position battle that followed in the area of the bridgehead continued until the following spring, when the Germans were forced to retreat after the collapse of the Cassino front. Also in this case, however, the main objective, that is the destruction of the German forces in Italy, was not achieved and the retreating Germans were able to escape the enemy's grip and rearrange themselves on the Gothic Line, a bulwark that engaged the Allies on the Apennines for months.

In January, despite the unfavorable weather conditions, TBF bombers constantly pounded the Italian railroad system. Their efforts were concentrated on the central part of the Italian peninsula. The main targets hit were Ancona, Arezzo, Fabriano, Foligno, Grosseto, Lucca, Pontedera, Siena, and the railway bridges of Orvieto and Giulianova. In all, the medium bombers scored 340 sorties on these targets.

On January 29, while the 8th Air Force from England bombed Nazi Germany with approximately 863 B-17 and B-24 bombers, dropping nearly 2,000 tons of bombs on Frankfurt, in Italy the 15th Air Force sent B-17 and B-24s against the railway stations of Ancona, Siena, Fabriano, Prato and Rimini.

In the first three weeks preceding the Anzio landing, the XII ASC aircraft had made over 5,500 sorties, mostly flown by fighters and fighter-bombers, in close support of the Fifth Army, with a total ordnance load of 5,400 tons. Their main targets included the road junctions at Cassino and Cervaro, the construction sites at Aquino and Ceccano, the railroad and roads at Formia and Fondi, the important junction at Frosinone on Highway 6, some roads at Sora and the entrance to a tunnel at Terracina.

On January 31, the high presence of enemy aircraft on the airports of northern Italy led the 15th Air Force to raise heavy four-engine aircraft from the runways of Puglia. Forty-one B-24 Liberators bombed the airport of Aviano, while 70 B-17 Flying Fortress bombed the airport of Udine. At the same time the XII ASC sent the A-36A, P-40 and P-47 over roads, junctions and the small towns of the Apennines. A-20 Havoc light twin-engine aircraft also participated in the actions. On February 2, Brigadier General P. Saville, who took the place of Major General J. House, took command of the XII ASC, but the strategy would remain almost unchanged.

In the period from the landing at Anzio to 4 February, medium bombers flew a total of 45 missions, 24 of which the Germans depended on because of damage to the railway lines. Fifteen of these missions were aimed at creating roadblocks in the Colli Laziali area at the junctions of Frascati, Albano, Palestrina, Marino, Mancini, Lariano, and Genzano.

▲ The Bristol Beaufighter Mk VIF "Honeychile" of the 416th Night Fighter Squadron USAAF, pictured here at Grottaglie on 17 November 1943. On the right is a pair of Martin 187 Baltimore.

▼ Capodichino airport and Vesuvius volcano photographed during the eruption in March 1944.

▲ From left: Major General Nathan F. Twining, commander of the 15th Air Force, General Ira C. Eaker, commander of MAAF, and Major General Joseph Cannon, commander of 12th Air Support Command, photographed during a meeting held in Caserta on Jan. 21, 1944.

▼ U.S. President Franklin Delano Roosevelt visiting Italy, here seated in a Willys Jeep with General Mark Clark, commander of the U.S. 5th Army, to his right.

▲ Italian workers supervised by American personnel are loading 1,000-pound aerial bombs onto a truck. Photo taken at the Port of Naples on November 6, 1943.

▼ Italian civilians work to clear the rubble caused by Allied bombing in Naples.

▲ Gunners from the 79th FG are preparing ribbon links with 50-cal rounds, to be loaded on the group's P-40s. The Curtiss P-40 was equipped with six 12.7 mm Browning M2s.

▼ The German bombardment of the port of Bari occurred on December 2, 1943.

▲ U.S. servicemen walk over a carpet of bombs in the port of Bari, trying to extinguish several fires.

▼ Civilians wounded in Luftwaffe bombing of Bari.

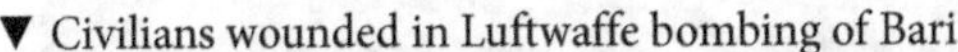

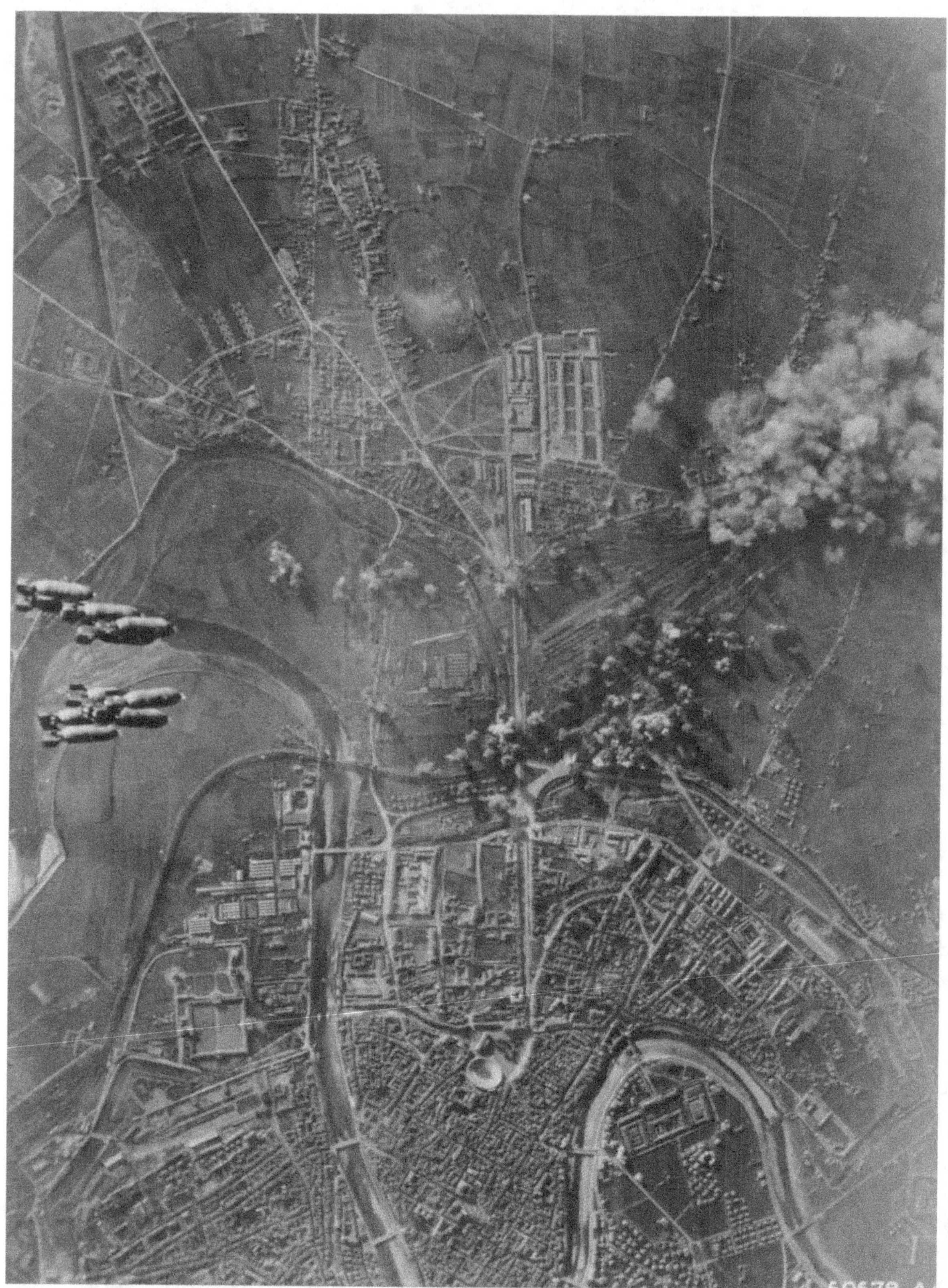

▲ Bombs dropped on the Verona train station. The American B-17s made their first appearance here on 30 December 1943. At the bottom of the photo the Arena of Verona is clearly visible.

▲ On December 30, 1943 a formation of Boeing B-17 Flying Fortresses attacked the Rimini train station. The first American bombing raid on this location was carried out on November 1, 1943 by B-25s of the 47th Bombardment Wing.

▼ Bombs launched from B-17s are about to hit the industrial area of Turin.

The Fiat factory in Turin hit during the raid of December 1, 1943. On that occasion the 118 B-17s of the 15th Air Force dropped about 354 tons of ordnance on the plant. The P-38 Lightning air escort had to face about 30 Luftwaffe aircraft, shooting down two of them and damaging three others.

The industrial area of Turin, Italy, bombed on November 8, 1943 by a formation of 81 B-17s of the 15th Air Force, which dropped 732 500 lb. high explosive devices.

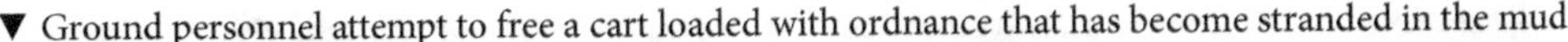

▲ Pisa railway station attacked on Christmas Day 1943 by 60 B-26 Marauders. About 97 tons of ordnance were dropped on the target.

▼ Ground personnel attempt to free a cart loaded with ordnance that has become stranded in the mud.

▲ A formation of B-25 Mitchells of the 340th BG in flight. In the foreground is the B-25 s/n 42-32304.

▼ Bombs are dropped on the city of Prato. On January 15, 1944 the city and the railway station were heavily bombed by the B-24 Liberator of the 15th Air Force. In the same month two other bombings followed, on 21 and 29. In the center of the photo the central station with its monumental fountain.

▲ A perfect attack by B-26 Marauders on a road bridge between Orvieto and Florence.

▲ Bombing of a railway viaduct at Recco (GE), between Genoa and La Spezia. The two pictures show the before and after of the bombing by the B-17 Flying Fortress.

▼ The infrastructure of the port of Genoa destroyed by bombing. The Lanterna of Genoa escaped the bombings.

▲ Major Leon Gray of the 90th Photographic Wing USAAF, here posing in front of his F-5 "67" reconnaissance aircraft s/n 42-13067. He was the most decorated aerial reconnaissance pilot of the 3rd Photographic Reconnaissance Group. He lived to the age of 94, dying on November 26, 2007.

▲ A sunken ship in the port of Naples.

▼ Ordnance is dragged for loading onto a B-25 Mitchell.

FROM CASSINO TO ROME

On October 4, 1943, Alexander had met Eisenhower optimistically expecting to enter Rome by the end of October 1943, but (as we have just seen) things went differently. The same day the Gustav Line was prepared, with Hitler's disposition. Kesselring succeeded in his intent by allowing the engineers to complete the fortification of two main defensive lines south of Rome: one, more to the south called Bernhardt Line or Winter Line for the Allies (Winter Line), and a second line that exploiting the Apennines and the course of the rivers, with its base in the Liri Valley cut in half the Peninsula in its narrowest section. This line was called Gustav Line, and its route went from the Gulf of Gaeta, on the Tyrrhenian Sea, to the city of Ortona, on the Adriatic Sea; its center of gravity was located on the massif of Monte Cassino. It was conceived as a field and semi-permanent defensive system; in the valley mobile steel casemates were installed, as well as concrete structures, while in the mountainous area defensive works were erected, such as stone posts and shelters, exploiting natural cavities enlarged by means of pneumatic hammers, explosives or often using simple manual tools. The workers were initially recruited with coercive methods among the local population, to which were added Alsatians, Slovenes, Russians, Poles, Romanians and obviously Germans.

From the landing at Anzio until the beginning of March, the Fifth Army had hammered the Gustav Line in a courageous but futile attempt to break through, to rejoin the forces at Anzio. On Sunday, February 13, the "Corriere della Sera" warned in an article dated Rome February 12, that "this morning the enemy propaganda insisted on the false claim that the Germans have transformed the Abbey of Montecassino into a fortified center. Reuter tries to mask the failure of the Allied attacks in the area of Cassino by claiming that it is defended by the machine guns placed between the walls of the Abbey, machine guns that would have opened fire on the American infantry, while the Allied artillery could not have intervened in order not to hit the monumental and historic work of art. The reality is that the enemy is afraid of assuming a tremendous responsibility by destroying one of the most important monuments of Christianity and once again tries, with lies, to place the blame on the Germans"[22].

At 9:00 a.m. on February 15, 24 hours after the launch of leaflets over Cassino urging people to leave the monastery immediately, a first wave of American bombers arrived over the abbey of Montecassino. By noon, B-17s, B-25s, and B-26s had dropped hundreds of bombs. Just 142 B-17s that had taken part in the raid had dropped 576 tons of high explosives. The heavy war effort would not, however, lead to the retreat of the Germans, who continued to hold on to strategic outposts.

In a broader context, at the end of February, Europe saw the implementation of Operation Argument, a large-scale air offensive undertaken by the RAF and USAAF from 20 to 25 February 1944, also nicknamed Big Week[23]. The target was the seventeen major aircraft factories and twenty major airports in Germany. The major effort was supported by the

---

22 Marco Patricelli, *op. cit.*, p. 297.

23 15th Air Force aircraft dropped 303,842 tons of bombs on enemy targets in 12 different European countries during the European operational cycle.

United States Strategic Air Forces (USSTAF), which also availed itself of the fighter escort of the British Fighter Command, but some night actions were also carried out by the Bomber Command. Among them were also the bombers of the 15th Air Force in Italy. Despite the efforts of the Allied air forces, Adolf Hitler's industry did not suffer the drop in production that the Allied commanders had imagined.

On March 15, the largest air operation in that theater up to that date was carried out: more than 1,000 Allied planes riddled the monastery of Montecassino and the nearby defensive positions of the German army with bombs, on which they dropped more than 1,200 tons of bombs. The air forces of the 12th and 15th Air Forces engaged 275 heavy bombers and nearly 200 medium bombers, dropping more than 2,000 pounds of bombs. Although the Benedictine monastery was completely demolished, the attack was yet another failure. In the night between 14 and 15, a rare offensive action by the Luftwaffe occurred over Naples, killing 146 people.

With the arrival of spring, the air operations of the Mediterranean Allied Air Forces (MAAF) increased in intensity. On 19 March, the official start of Operation Strangle was given, which had the aim of hindering and suffocating all movements and supplies destined for the German troops who were feeding the Gustav Line. Thus, all railroad and road bridges of tactical interest were systematically hit one after the other.

On March 22, about one hundred B-24s bombed the railroad stations of Bologna and Rimini; an equally large number of B-17s targeted the Verona railroad station. B-25s and B-26s of the 12th Air Force bombed a road bridge near Poggibonsi and a viaduct in Arezzo. The stunning eruption of the volcano Vesuvius, and the ensuing rain of lapilli, destroyed about 88 B-25 Mitchells of the 340th Bombardment Group on the Pompeii airfield.

On Tuesday, March 28, four hundred B-17s and B-24s hit Verona, Mestre, Fano, and the bridges at the mouth of the Cesano and Fano rivers. On the 29th, another 405 B-17s and B-24s shared the targets of Turin, Bolzano and Milan.

Medium bombers flew 176 missions against railway targets, 113 of which against targets on the Florence-Rome line. This was certainly the most important line in central Italy, so much so that it was attacked at twenty-two different points between Florence and Orte; nineteen of these bombed targets included bridges.

The climax of the strategic campaign materialized in a series of seven missions carried out over five days by the 15th Air Force in late March. Three of the attacks - on the 22nd, 28th and 29th - were particularly heavy, involving the bombers in a total of almost 1,000 sorties. On the 28th the first 1,000-ton sortie by 15th Air Force aircraft was carried out by the bombers of the 2nd, 97th, 98th, 99th, 301st, 376th, 449th, 450th, 451st, 454th, 455th, 456th and 459th Bombardment Groups. The seven raids caused severe damage to railroad yards and industrial targets in Verona, Mestre, Turin, Bolzano, Milan, Bologna and Rimini.

At about 13:00 on the 7th of April, Good Friday, the city of Treviso was hit by an avalanche of fire from the sky, emitted by a hundred B-17s coming from the bases in Puglia. The attack destroyed almost the entire city, causing the death of more than 1,500 people. In the same day the B-24 bombed the railway stations of Bologna and Mestre.

During the month heavy attacks were carried out on the cities of Ancona, Castelfranco Veneto, Padua, Vicenza, Venice, Mestre, Monfalcone and Trieste. On 25 April, about one hundred and fifty Liberators attacked the aeronautical factories in Turin and tactical targets in Parma and Ferrara.

On the 28th Piombino, Santo Stefano a Mare and Orbetello were heavily hit. On May 2, more than 250 aircraft of the 15th Air Force, including B-17s and B-24s, bombed Bolzano, Castel Maggiore and a railway bridge near Faenza.

Operation Strangle ended on May 11 and was undoubtedly a great success; a few days later, on May 19, all of Cassino was already in Allied hands. In the operations conducted by the 15th Air Force during Strangle, heavy bombers dropped more than 5,000 tons of bombs on the communication routes. From March 19 to May 11, MAAF operations against lines of communication and ports totaled about 50,000 sorties, with a total of about 26,000 tons of bombs dropped.

In the month of April 1944 Clark, strongly shaken after the repeated failures of the ground troops, had secretly returned to the United States where he remained for two weeks; the American leaders illustrated to the General the plans of the planned Allied planning for the so-called Operation Overlord, the great landing in France planned for June 5th. They also underlined that it would have been propagandistically important that before that date the American troops had succeeded in liberating Rome. Clark, still determined to conquer Rome out of personal ambition, returned to Italy determined to launch a new offensive. At the same time, also Winston Churchill and Alexander were intent on resuming operations against the Gustav Line, code-named Operation Diadem, in such a way as to coincide with the landing of Normandy in France; this would have led to a weakening of the German forces on several fronts.

It was decided that the Polish II Corps, the British XIII Corps, belonging to the Eighth Army, the French Corps Expéditionnaire (including the Moroccan Goumier) and the II Corps of the American Fifth Army would be employed.

Operation Diadem kicked off at 23:00 hours on May 11, 1944. The British XIII Corps forced a crossing over the Rapido River in the Liri Valley against strong opposition from local German reserves. The Corps Expéditionnaire Français pushed their opponents back into the mountains on the left front on 14 May, supported along the coast by II Corps of the United States. On May 17, the Polish II Corps attacked Mount Cassino on the right.

The German position collapsed, and the Germans had to abandon the Gustav Line and fall back to the Hitler Line, about 10 miles (16 kilometers) away. This struggle caused the German reserves to move from that position, thus reducing the pressure on the bridgehead at Anzio.

On May 12, the largest air formation that had ever flown over the skies of Italy, consisting of Flying Fortresses and Liberators, made 1,143 sorties, dropping 1,912 tons of bombs as part of Operation Diadem. The German headquarters at Massa d'Albe and Monte Soratte, the city of Civitavecchia, the airports of Tarquinia, Chivasso, Piombino, Marina di Carrara, Viareggio, Ferrara, Santo Stefano al Mare, Chiavari, La Spezia and the airport of Piacenza, were attacked. There were more than two hundred and fifty fighters in support of the operations. The following day, Saturday the 13th, 670 B-17 and B-24 fighters, heavily escorted, attacked Trento, Fidenza, Piacenza, Faenza, Imola, Cesena, Modena, Parma, San Rufillo, Borgo San Lorenzo, Castel Maggiore, Bologna, Bolzano and Modena. On the 14th, over seven hundred four-engine aircraft, escorted by over 170 fighters, headed for Ferrara, Mantua and Piacenza; the B-17s for Vicenza; and the B-24s for Piacenza and Reggio Emilia. Heavy bombardments were repeated throughout the month. On the 28th it was also the turn of Genoa and Vercelli.

The Hitler Line was violated on 23 May in Pontecorvo by the First Canadian Infantry Division. The 10th Army of the Wehrmacht was then forced to retreat towards the northwest. Major General Lucian K. Truscott's VI Corps, moving from Anzio to the northeast, was on the verge of cutting off the German line of retreat, but the commander of the U.S. Fifth Army, General Mark Wayne Clark, inexplicably ordered them to advance toward Rome instead of turning northwest to pursue the enemy. It is said that Clark implemented this maneuver to get his own personal gratification for liberating Rome. The consequence, however, was that General Heinrich von Vietinghoff's German 10th Army was able to retreat without suffering further losses. The Germans, after having fought a series of delaying actions, withdrew on the Albert Line (or Trasimeno Line) and then on the Gothic Line, north of the Arno river. After the breakthrough of the sector of Cassino and of the sector of the Anzio and Nettuno landing head, the German commander Kesselring put in feet a retreat of his forces on the Gothic Line, abandoning therefore Rome. The capital was finally liberated on 4 June 1944 by the US Fifth Army, coming from the Tyrrhenian sector. On the same day the 15th Air Force continued its bombing raids on Genoa, Novi Ligure, Savona and Turin; while fighter-bombers of the 12th ASC attacked over 600 retreating German vehicles on the roads north of Rome.

▲ The crew of a B-26 from the 15th Air Force celebrates 8,000,000 pounds of bombs dropped.

▲ The rubble of Cassino photographed by an American F-5 scout.

▼ The shadow of a Lockheed F-5 on the Latium coast, near Sabaudia. On the right is the barracks of the School of Anti-Aircraft Artillery, no longer in existence.

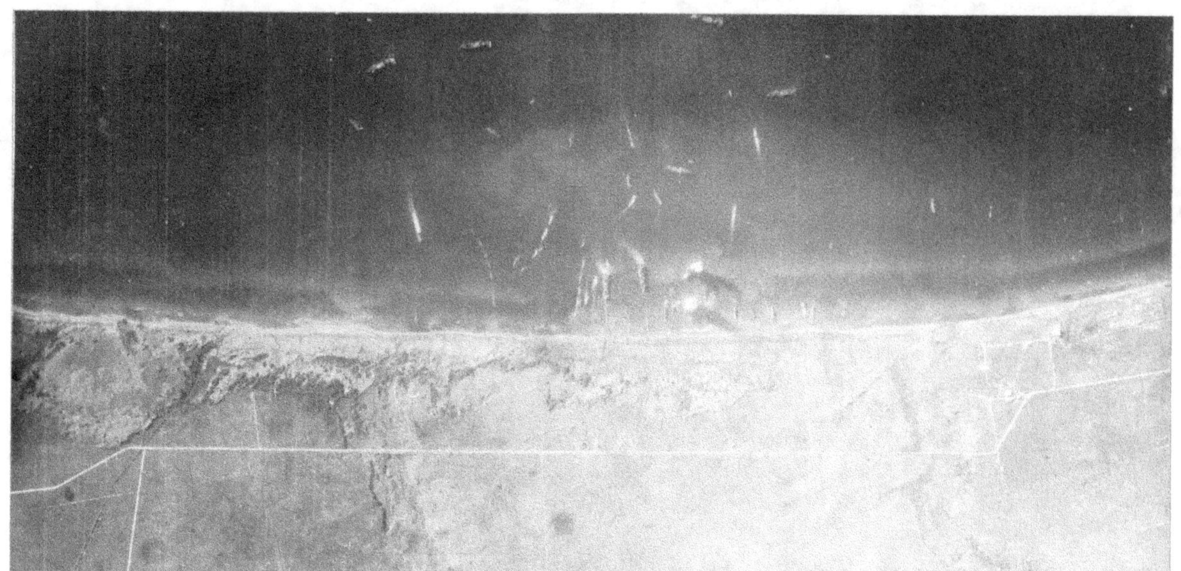

▲ The landing at Anzio (codenamed Operation Shingle) photographed on January 22, 1944 by an F-5 reconnaissance aircraft of the 12th USAAF Photographic Reconnaissance Squadron.

▼ The bombardment of the port of Piombino. During the night between January 10 and 11, the city suffered its first heavy bombardment by B-26s of the XII Bomber Command. This photo refers in all probability to the bombing carried out on March 20, 1944 by the B-26 of the XII BC.

▲ The port of Civitavecchia attacked by B-25 Mitchell.

▼ The port infrastructure of Civitavecchia destroyed by Allied bombing.

▲ The port of Civitavecchia reduced to a pile of rubble.

▼ A railroad bridge destroyed during Operation Strangle.

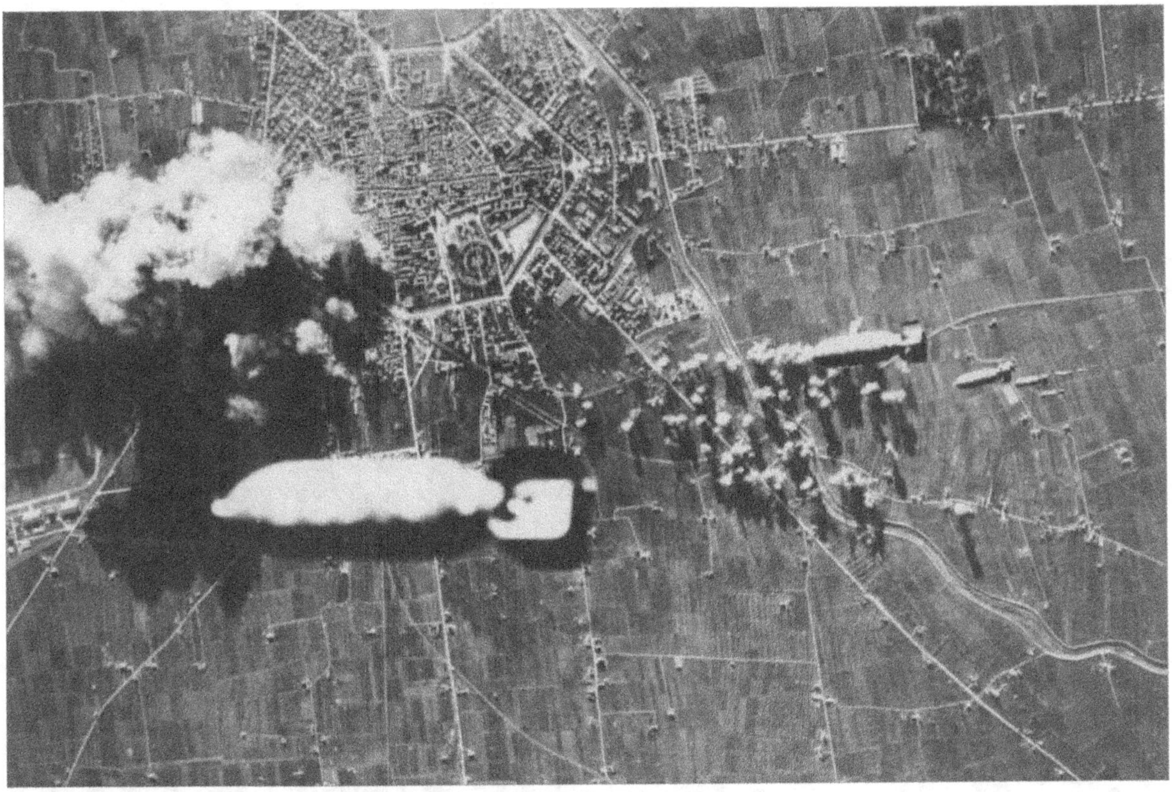

▲ First bombing raid by B-17s on Reggio Emilia on December 29, 1943.

▼ The railway station of Reggio Emilia destroyed by bombing.

▲ The warehouses of the public transport depot destroyed by the bombing of Reggio Emilia.

▼ Ground personnel are hooking up a 500-lb ordnance on a P-40 Warhawk from the 79th FG at Capodichino Airport, Naples.

▲ The before, during and after of the attack on a bridge near San Donà di Piave.

▲ Some B-25 Mitchells just attacked targets near Terni. B-17s attacked the city on August 11 and 28, and October 21, 1943. The last American bombing raid on Terni was carried out on April 24, 1944, by aircraft of the Tactical Air Force.

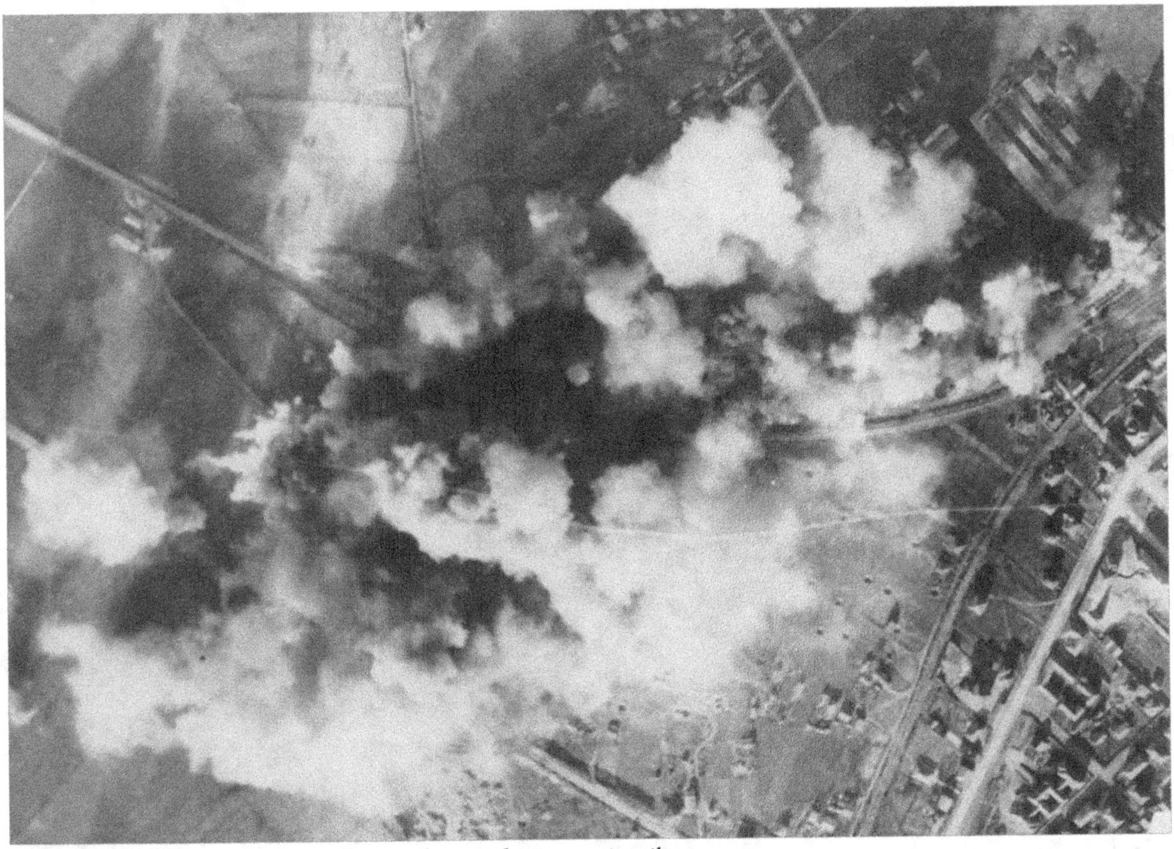

▲ Avezzano shrouded in smoke from explosions during an airstrike.

▼ Two B-25 Mitchells drop their ordnance on an unspecified location.

▲ German armored vehicles transported on a train are photographed by an American scout near Pescara.

▼ U.S. soldiers are inspecting some wrecked roadside vehicles near Rome.

▲ American vehicles cross the city of Viterbo destroyed by bombing.

▼ Cassino covered by explosions.

▲ Image taken at low altitude over the port of Ancona. The ship at lower right sunk on its side is the cruiser Ottaviano Augusto, sunk in the bombardment of November 1, 1943. The ship burned on the quay is instead the Regia Nave Savoia.

▼ The Allies cross the city of Arezzo.

▲ The railway station of Arezzo damaged by the bombardments.

▼ The industrial area of Livorno completely destroyed by bombing.

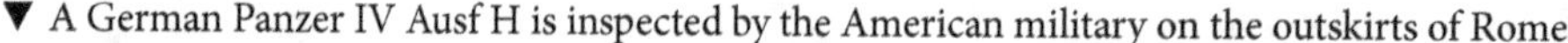

▲ The city of Livorno seen from the perspective of the port. Note the numerous sunken vessels and the completely destroyed port infrastructure.

▼ A German Panzer IV Ausf H is inspected by the American military on the outskirts of Rome.

Bibliography

- Alberti Agostino, Annoni Matteo, Da Cassino alla linea gotica. Le operazioni alleate sull'Italia. 12 maggio-24 agosto 1944 Roma, IBN, 2017.
- Alberti Agostino, Merli Luca, Ali stellate sul Lazio. Il Lazio nel mirino della Twelfth Air Force dell'USAAF. Le operazioni tattiche del maggio 1944, Roma, IBN, 2021.
- Alberti Agostino, Merli Luca, Bombe sulla Linea Gustav. Le operazioni della Twelfth Air Force sull'Italia. Gennaio-aprile 1944, Roma, IBN, 2020.
- Alberti Agostino, Merli Luca, La Fifteenth Air Force dell'USAAF in azione sull'Italia. Gennaio-aprile 1944, Roma, IBN, 2020.
- Brookes Andrew, Air war over Italy, London, Ian Allan, 2000.
- Craven Wesley Frank, Cate James Lea, The Army Air Force in World War II vol. II, Chicago, University of Chicago Press, 1965.
- Craven Wesley Frank, Cate James Lea, The Army Air Force in World War II vol. III, Chicago, University of Chicago Press, 1965.
- Cristini Luca Stefano, La battaglia di Anzio – L'Operazione "Shingle" gennaio 1944, Zanica (BG), Soldiershop, 2019.
- D'Este Carlo, 1943. Lo sbarco in Sicilia, Milano, Mondadori, 1990.
- D'Este Carlo, Anzio e la battaglia per Roma, Gorizia, LEG, 2020.
- De Simone Cesare, Venti Angeli sopra Roma, Milano, Mursia, 1993.
- Duma Antonio, Quelli del Cavallino Rampante - Storia del 4° Stormo Caccia, Roma, Aeronautica Militare, 2007.
- Eduard Mark, Center for Air Force History, Aerial Interdiction: Air Power and the Land Battle in Three American Wars, Washington D.C.,1994.
- Fagone Salvo, Ricognitori su Husky. Il ruolo cruciale della ricognizione aerea e dell'Intelligence Ultra sulla Sicilia e sul Mediterraneo, Youcanprint, 2020.
- Fagone Salvo, Road to Rome – Scatti e memorie di un rhodesiano nella RAF, Zanica (BG), Soldiershop, 2021.
- Freeman Roger A., Osborne David, The B-17 Flying Fortress Story, London, Arms & Armour Press, 1998.
- Gillies Peter S., Major, Sicily. Analysis of a combined operations battle, Air Command and Staff College Air University Maxwell, USA, 1984.
- Goss Chris, Heinkel He 111: The Early Years - Fall of France, Battle of Britain and the Blitz, Barnsley, Frontline Books, 2016.
- Gribaudi Gabriella, Guerra totale. Tra bombe alleate e violenze naziste. Napoli e il fronte meridionale 1940-1944, Torino, Bollati Boringhieri, 2005,
- Halley James J., Squadrons of the Royal Air Force, UK, Air Britain Historians Ltd, 1985.
- Hamilton Nigel, Monty: Master of the Battlefield, 1942-1944, Milano, McGraw-Hill, 1984.

- Hammel Eric, Air War Europa. America's air war against Germany in Europe and North Africa. Chronology 1942-1945, California, Pacifica Press, 1994.
- Lottici Mauro, Marzilli Marco, Cassino. Immagini di una vittoria amara. Ediz. Illustrate, Youcanprint, 2019.
- Mattesini Francesco, Bari 1943: la seconda Pearl Harbor, Zanica (BG), Soldiershop, 2020.
- Mitchelhill-green David, Air War over North Africa: USAAF Ascendant, Rare Photographs From Wartime Archives, Barnsley, Pen & Sword, 2019.
- Molony C. J. C., The Mediterranean and Middle East Volume V: The Campaign in Sicily 1943 and the campaign in Italy 3rd September 1943 to 31st March 1944, London, H.M.S.O, 1973.
- Pace Steve, B-25 Mitchell Units of the MTO, Oxford, Osprey Publishing, 2002.
- Patricelli Marco, L'Italia sotto le bombe, Roma, Laterza editori, 2007.
- Pedriali Ferdinando, L'Italia nella guerra aerea - Da El Alamein alle spiagge della Sicilia, Roma, Aeronautica Militare, Ufficio storico, 2010.
- Pedriali Ferdinando, L'Italia nella guerra aerea – Dalla difesa della Sicilia all'8 settembre, Roma, Aeronautica Militare, Ufficio storico, 2014.
- Plumari Angelo, Operazione Husky. La Guerra nell'entroterra ennese, Regalbuto (EN), Euno Edizioni, 2019.
- Ragatzu Alessandro, Luftwaffe in Sardegna, Cagliari, Alisea Edizioni, 2010.
- Rust Kenn C., Twelfh Air Force story in World War II, Londra, Hersant, 1967.
- Santoni Alberto, Mattesini Francesco, La partecipazione tedesca alla guerra aeronavale nel Mediterraneo (1940-1945), Parma, Albertelli edizioni speciali, 2005.
- Shores Christopher, Massimello Giovanni, A History of the Mediterranean Air War 1940-1945: Tunisia and the End in Africa, November 1942-1943: Volume Three: Tunisia and the end in Africa, November 1942 - May 1943, London, Grub Street Publishing, 2016.
- Shores Christopher, Massimello Giovanni, A History of the Mediterranean Air War, 1940-1945 Volume 4: Sicily and Italy to the fall of Rome 14 May, 1943 - 5 June, 1944, London, Grub Street Publishing, 2018.
- Styling Mark, B-26 Marauder Units of the MTO, Oxford, Osprey Publishing, 2008.
- Versolato Giuseppe, Bombardamenti aerei degli alleati nel vicentino. 1943-1945, Vicenza, Gino Rosato Editore, 2005.

TITLES ALREADY PUBLISHING

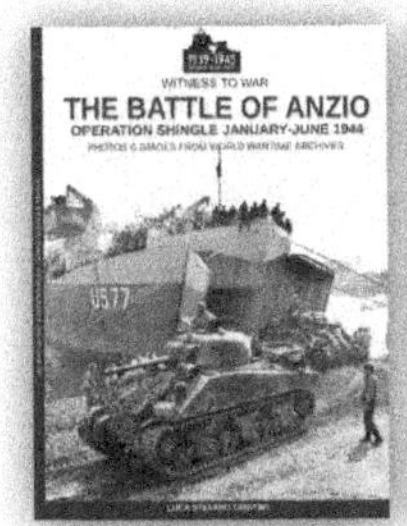

THE BATTLE OF ANZIO
OPERATION SHINGLE JANUARY-JUNE 1944

THE ALPINE TROOPS
IN THE ITALIAN SOCIAL REPUBLIC (R.S.I.)

THE TANKERS OF MUSSOLINI
ARMOURED GROUP "LEONESSA" FROM MVSN TO RSI

THE SHERMAN MEDIUM TANK
IN THE EUROPEAN THEATER OF OPERATIONS

REPARTI BERSAGLIERI NELLA R.S.I.

LE CINGOLETTE BRITANNICHE
DELLA SECONDA GUERRA MONDIALE

I REPARTI CORAZZATI ITALIANI NEI BALCANI 1941 - 1945

MILIZIA DIFESA TERRITORIALE E GUARDIE CIVICHE NELL'O.Z.A.K. 1943 -1945

**LE WAFFEN SS GERMANICHE SUL FRONTE ITALIANO.
LE DIVISIONI "REICHSFÜHRER" E "KARSTJÄGER"**

AERONAUTICA NAZIONALE REPUBBLICANA A.N.R. 1943-1945
L'EPICA LOTTA DELL'AVIAZIONE DELLA RSI

LE DIVISIONI DELL'E.N.R 1943 – 1945 VOLUME 1
1a DIVISIONE "ITALIA"
2a DIVISIONE "LITTORIO"

REPARTI CORAZZATI JUGOSLAVI 1940 -1945
REGNO DI JUGOSLAVIA - STATO INDIPENDENTE
DI CROAZIA - UNITÀ CROATE DELLA WEHRMACHT
DOMOBRANCI SLOVENI

LA DECISIONE DI MUSSOLINI DI OCCUPARE LA GRECIA
LA TRAGEDIA DELLE FORZE ARMATE ITALIANE E L'AIUTO
DELLA GERMANIA OTTOBRE 1940 - APRILE 1941

BARI 1943 LA SECONDA PEARL HARBOR
I BOMBARDAMENTI TEDESCHI SUI
PORTI DELL'ITALIA MERIDIONALE

BRESLAU 1945
L'ULTIMO BASTIONE DEL REICH

DALLA SICILIA AL SENIO
LA STRAORDINARIA STORIA DEL TENENTE
GIORGIO DE SANCTIS

LE CAMICIE NERE SUL FRONTE RUSSO 1941- 1943

LE ARTIGLIERIE DELLE FORZE ARMATE DELLA REPUBBLICA SOCIALE ITALIANA

**DIAVOLI BIANCHI!
IL BATTAGLIONE ALPINI SCIATORI "MONTE CERVINO" 1941- 1943**

IL GRUPPO DI COMBATTIMENTO LEGNANO

LA LANDSCHUTZ DEL LITORALE ADRIATICO

BAUTZEN 1945
L'ULTIMA VITTORIA DEL TERZO REICH

I REPARTI CORAZZATI DEL REGIO ESERCITO E L'ARMISTIZIO
3° VOLUME

I REPARTI CORAZZATI DEL REGIO ESERCITO E L'ARMISTIZIO
2° VOLUME

LE DIVISIONI DELL'E.N.R 1943 – 1945 VOLUME 2
3ª DIVISIONE "SAN MARCO"
4ª DIVISIONE "MONTEROSA"

BOOKS TO COLLECT